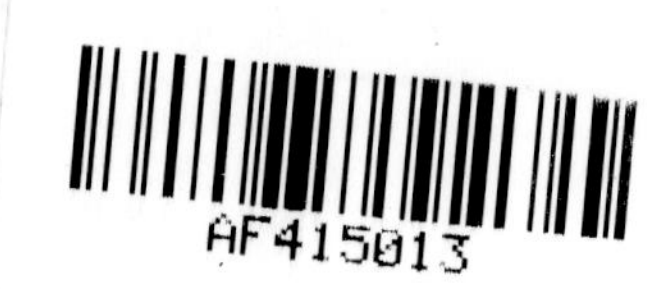

HALLOWEEN COLORING BOOK FOR ADULT

THIS HALLOWEEN COLORING BOOK BELONGS TO

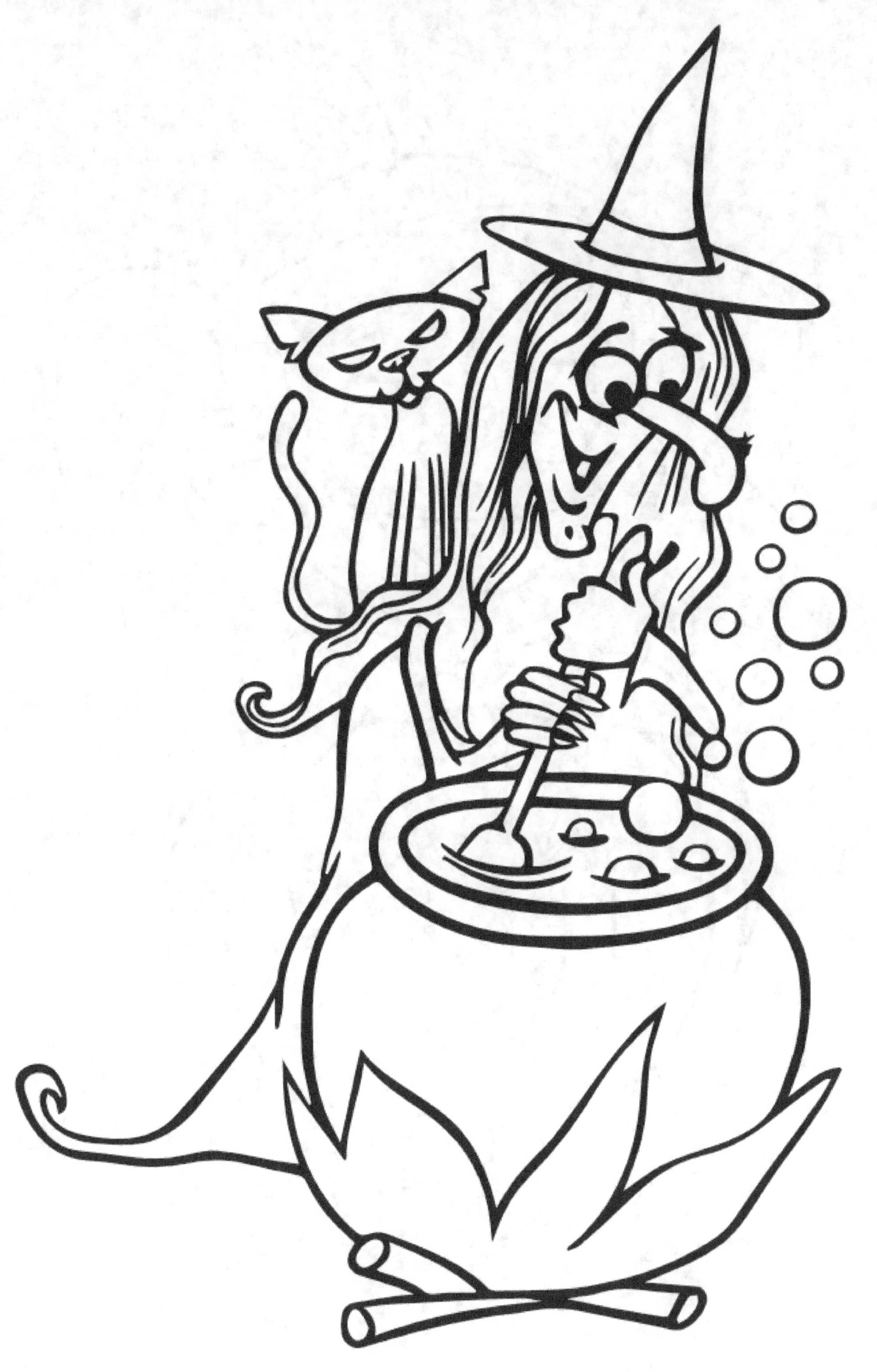

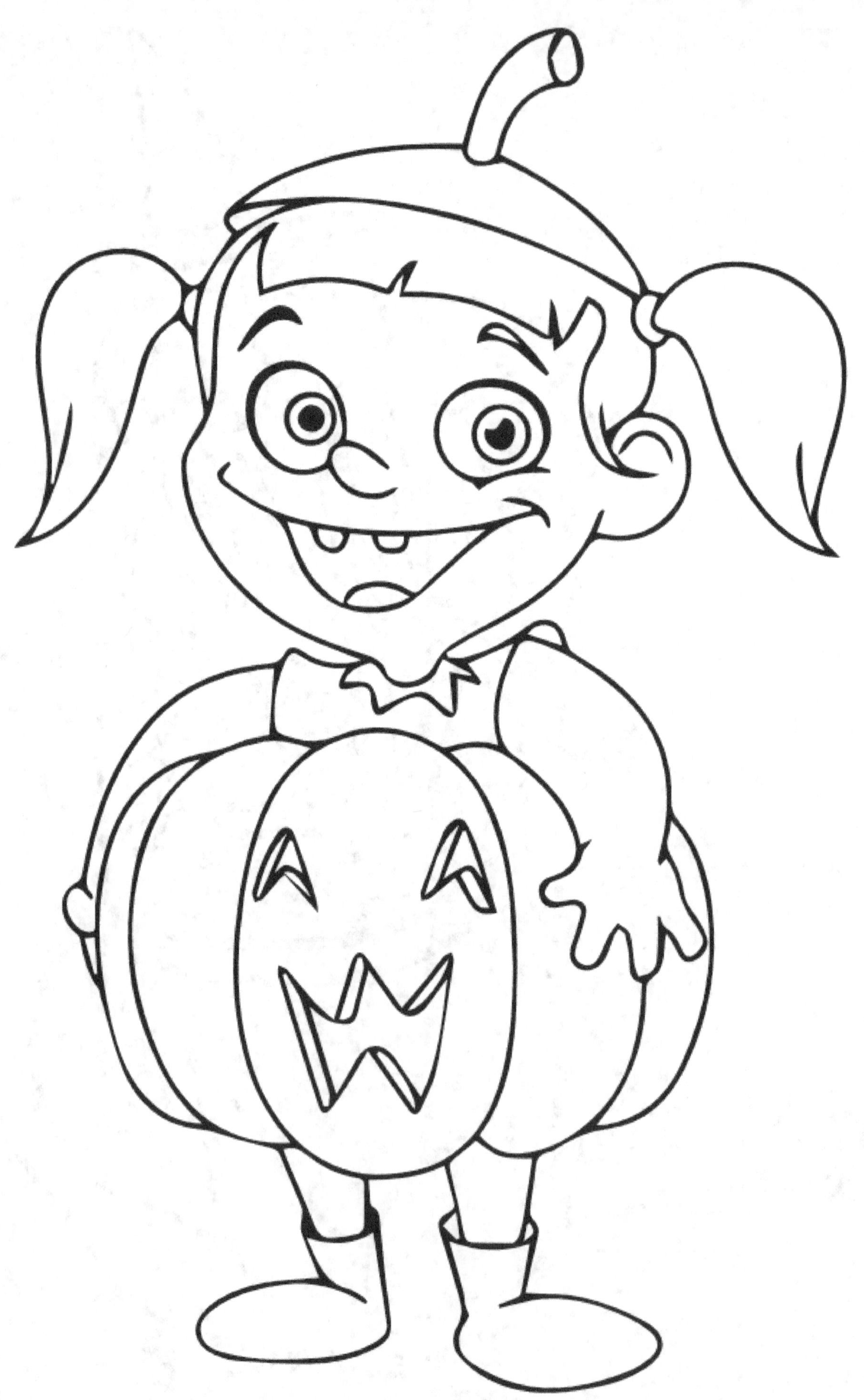

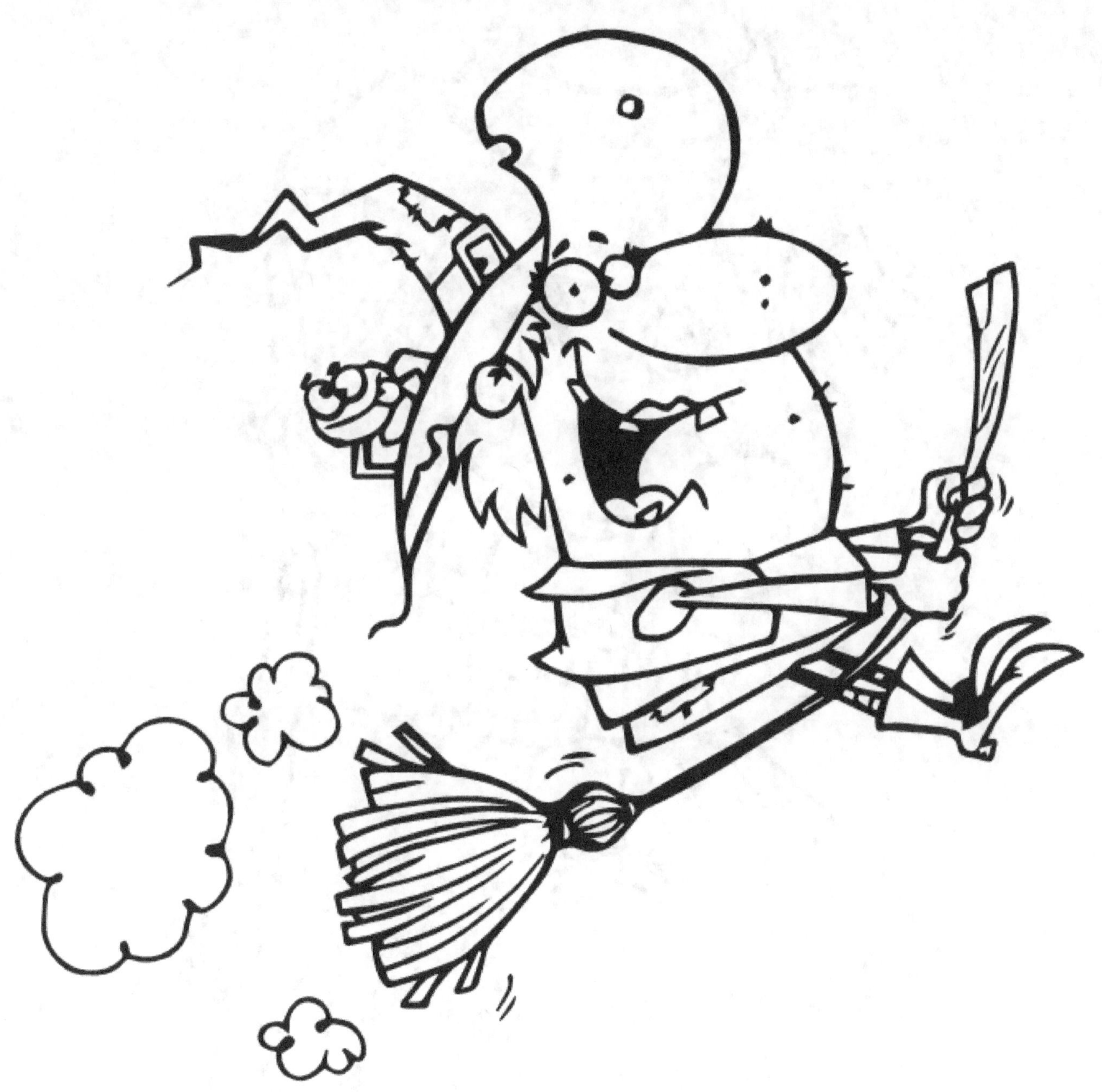

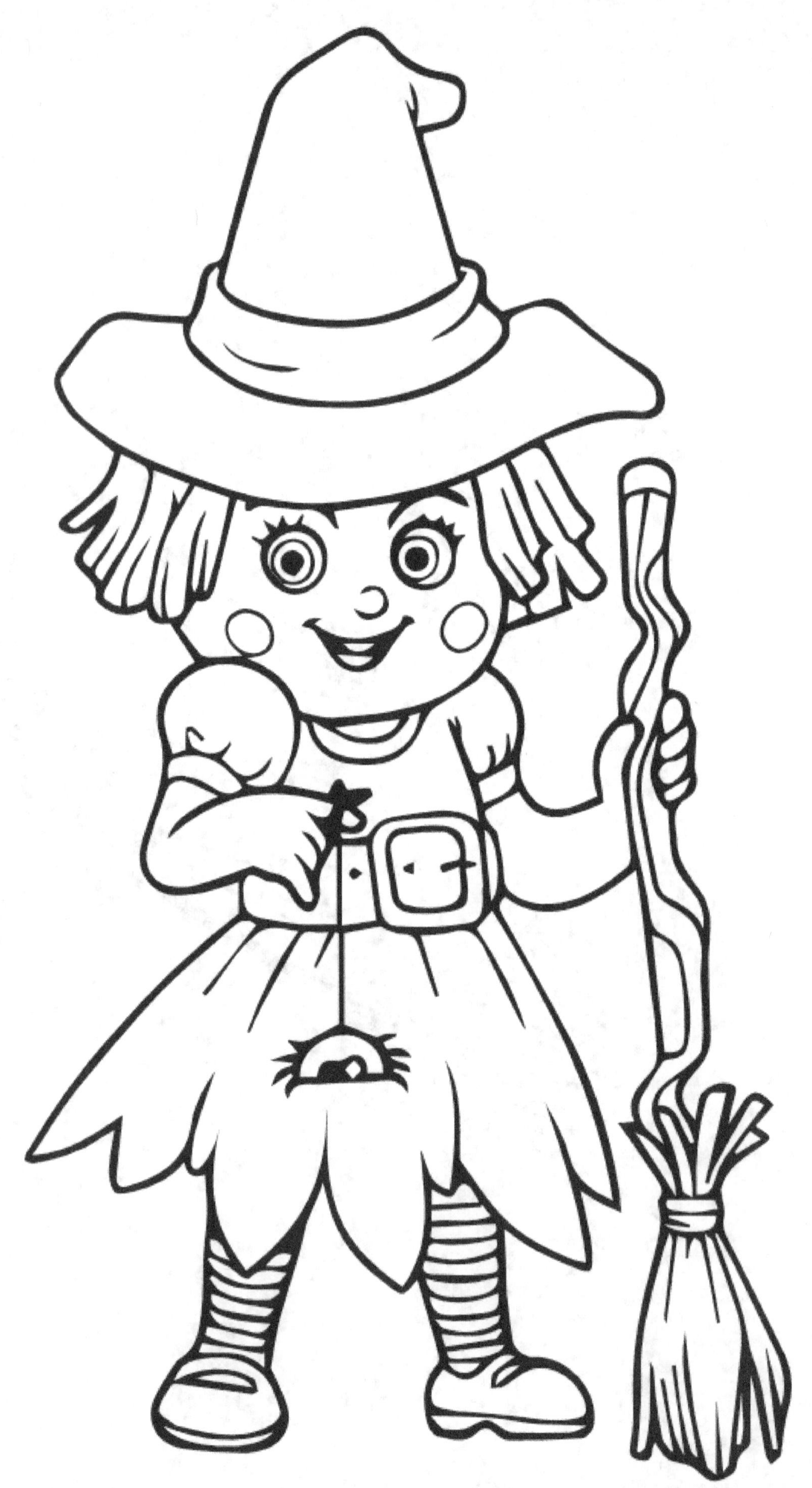

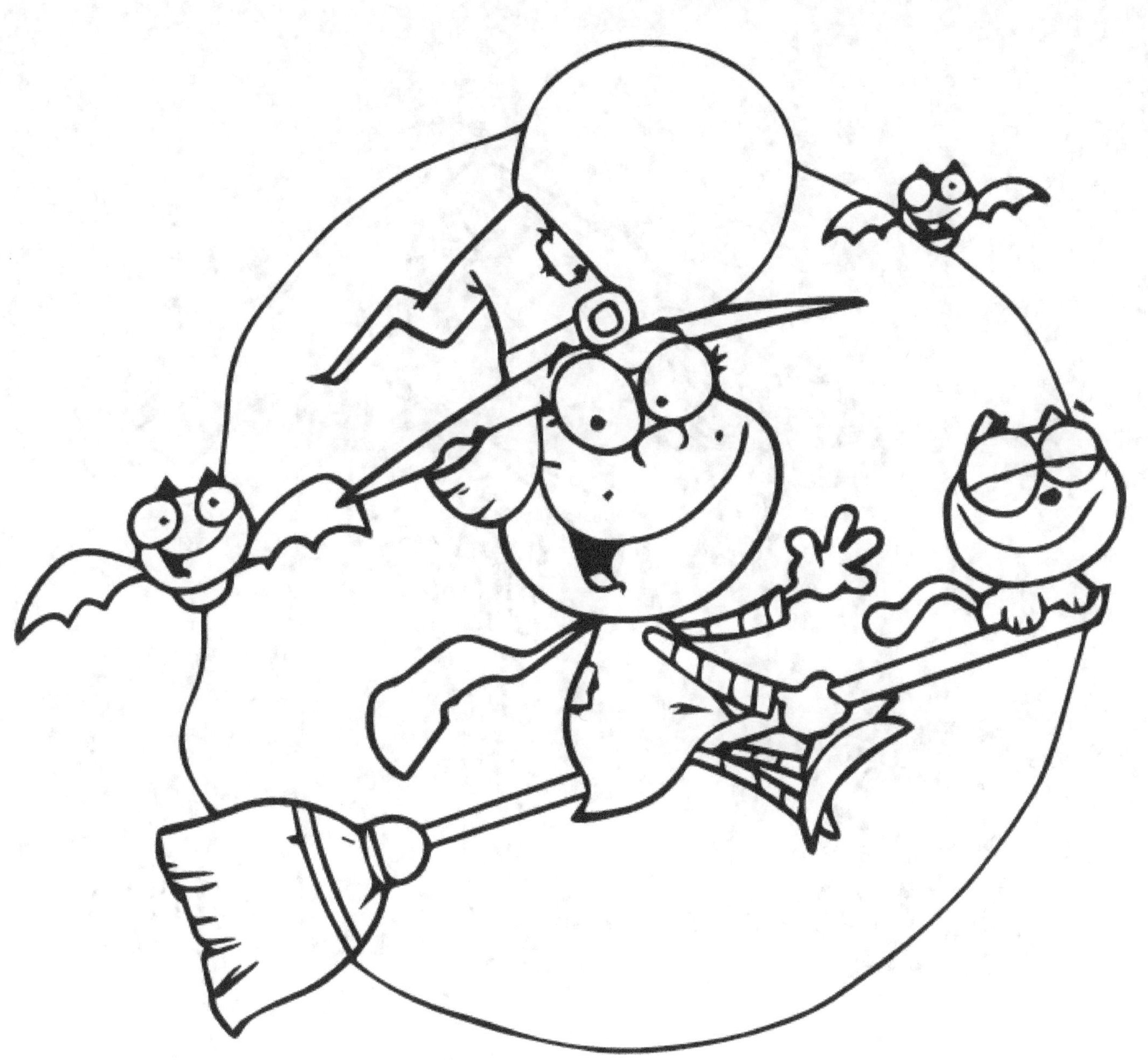

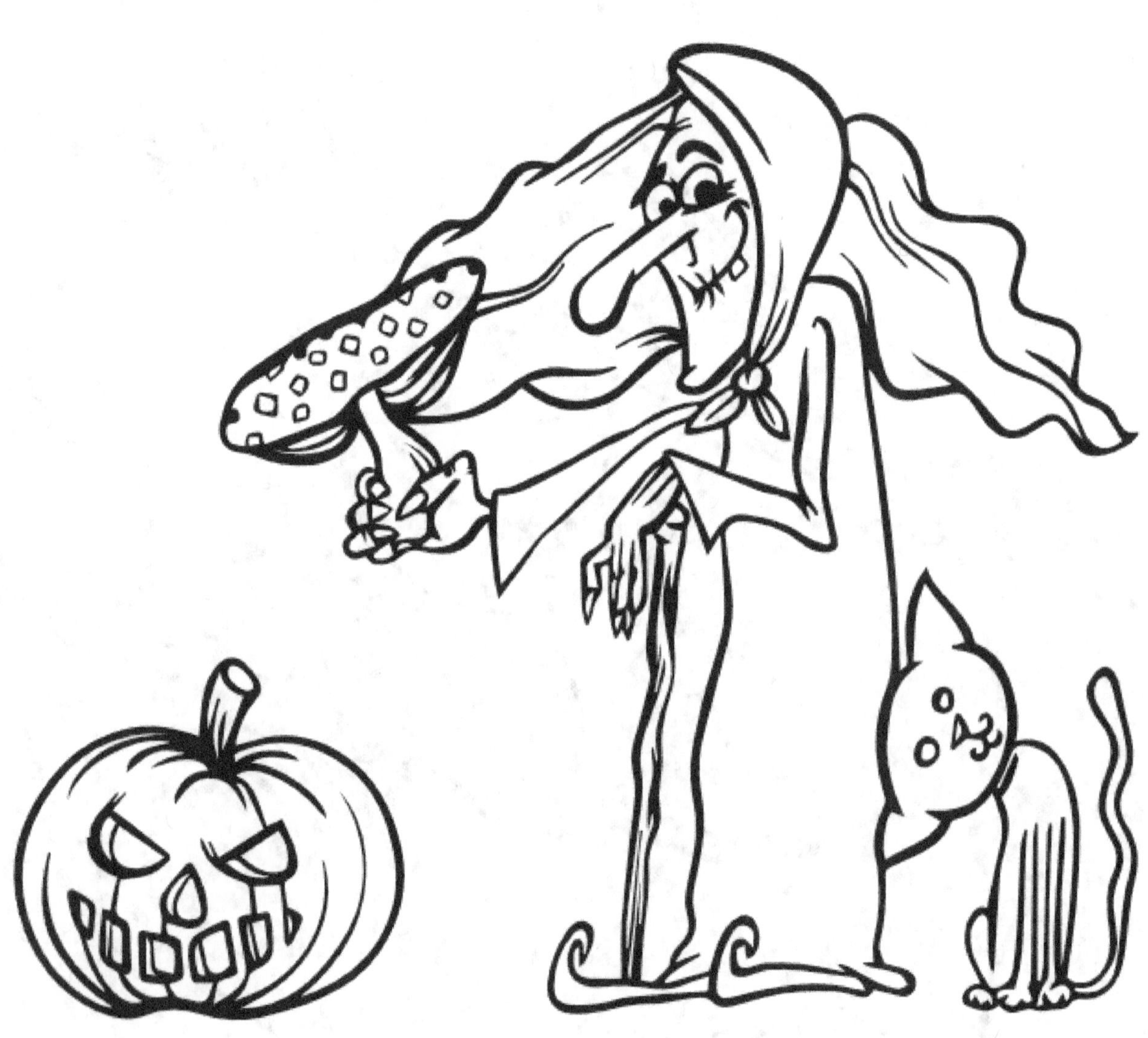

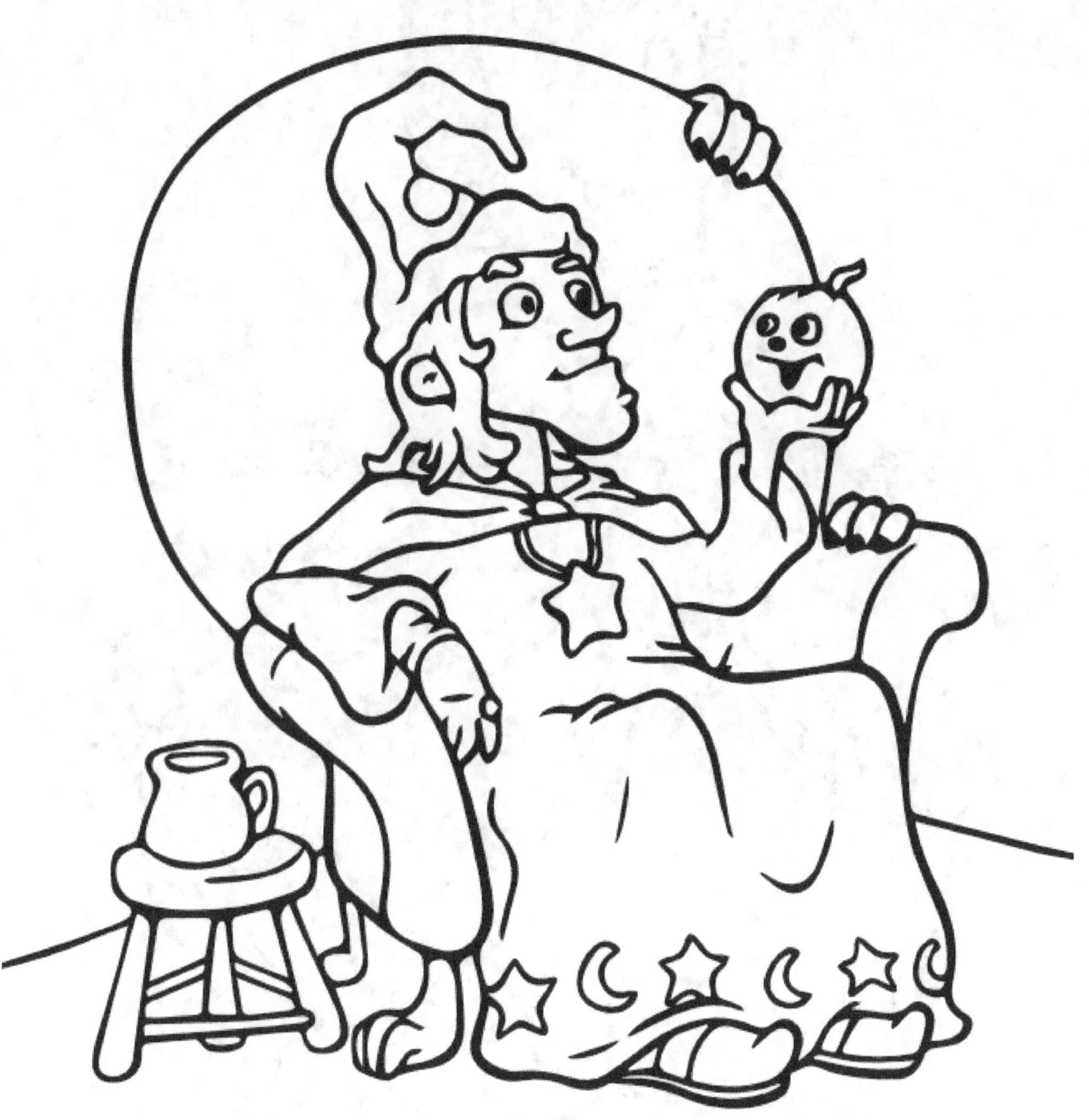

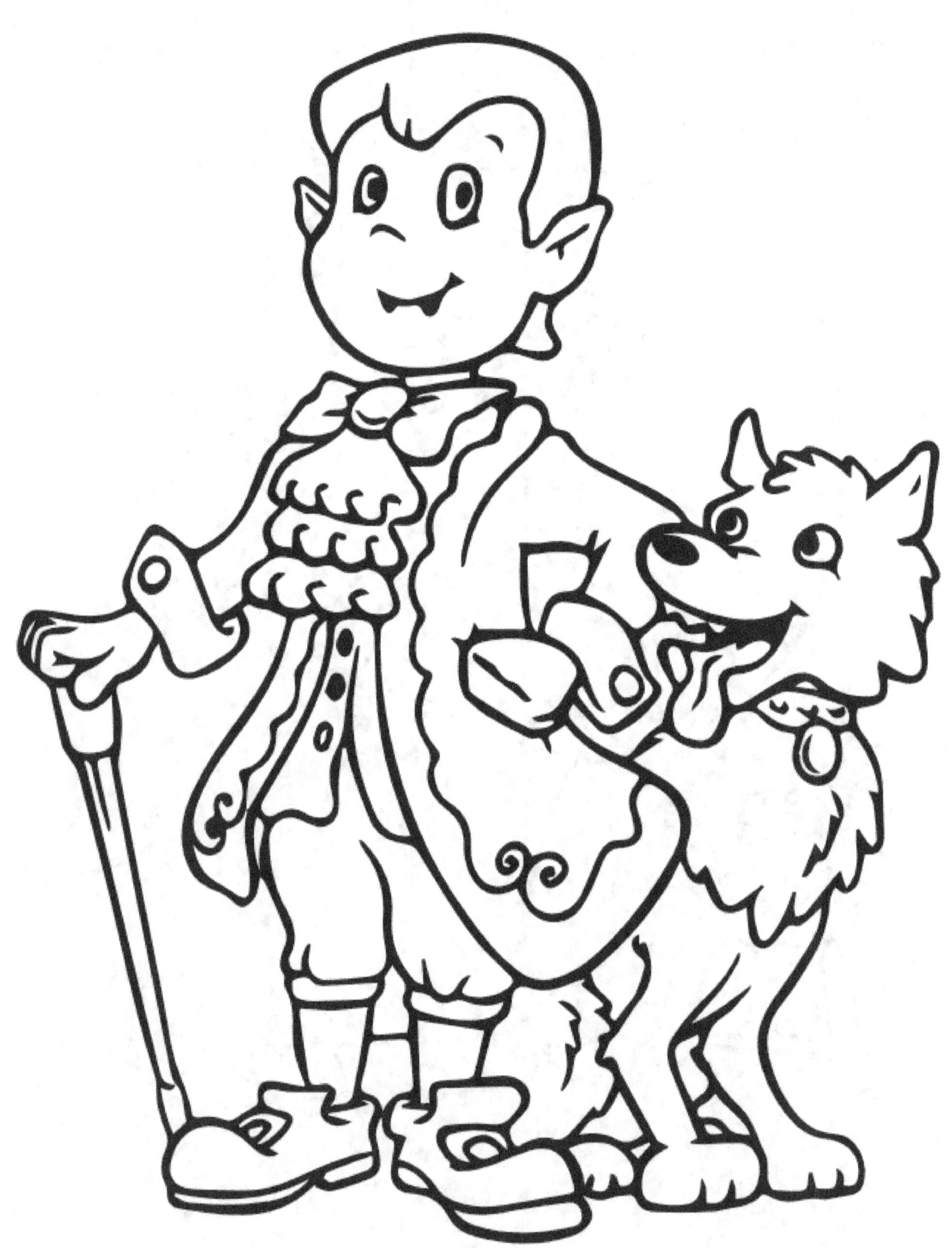

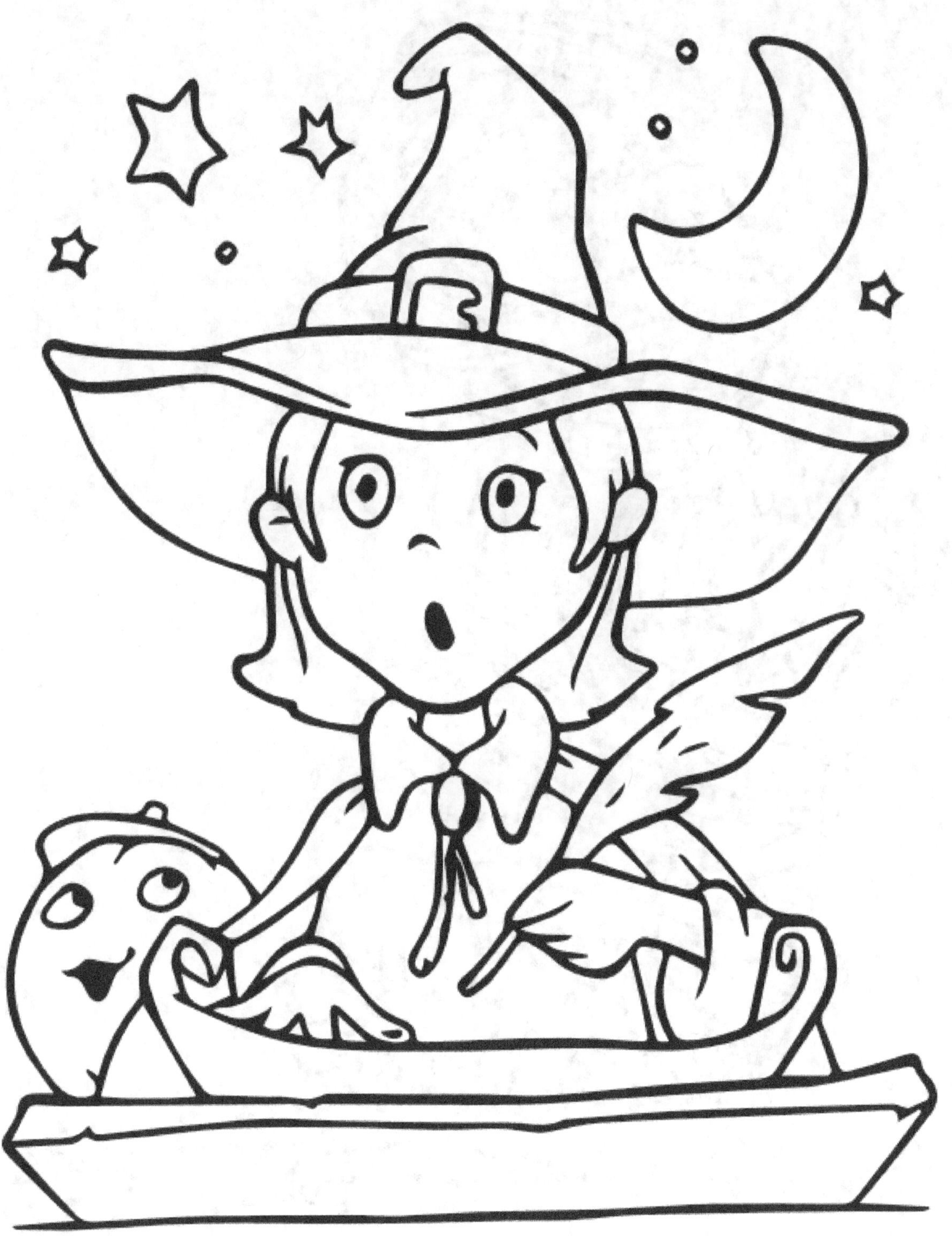

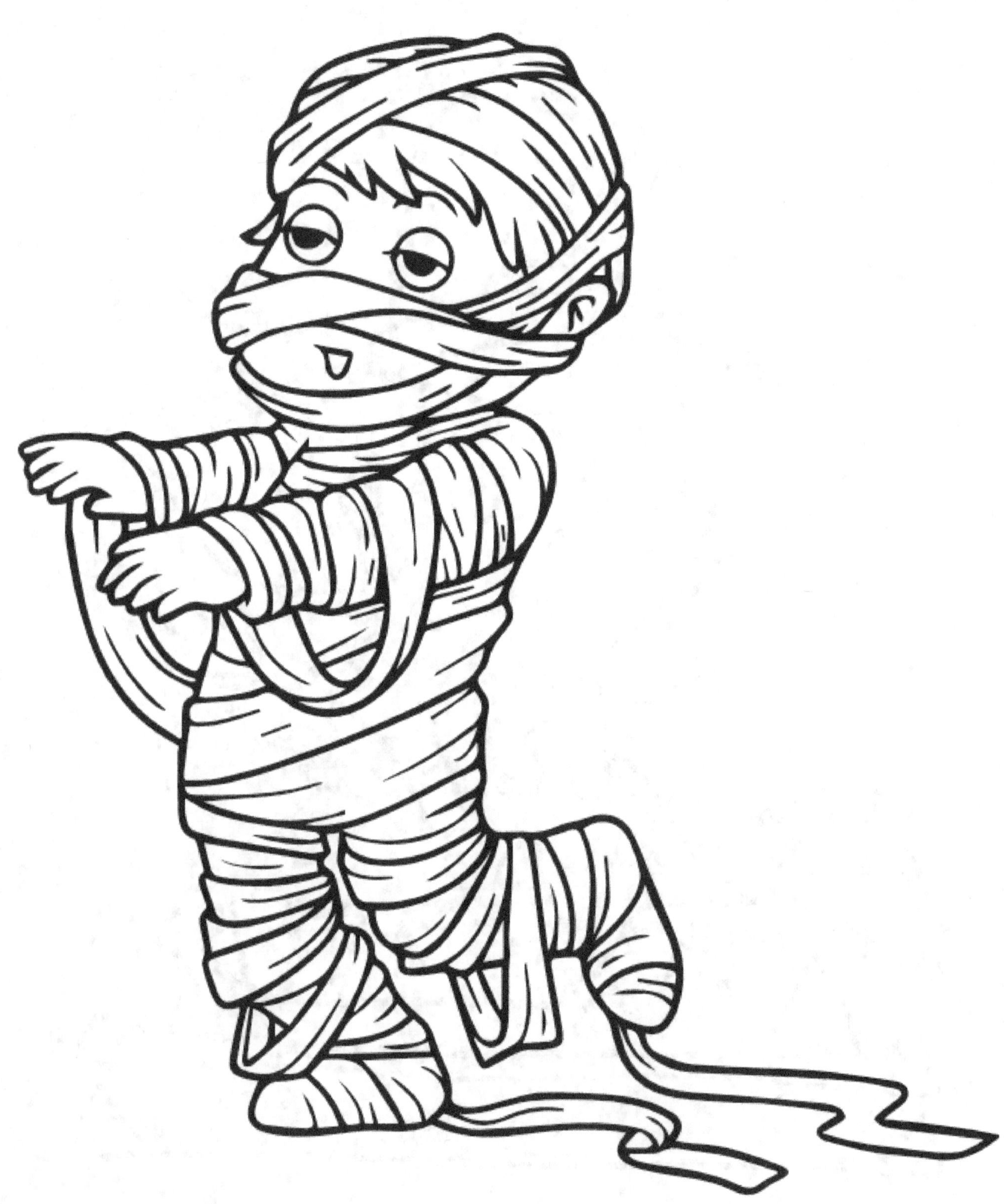

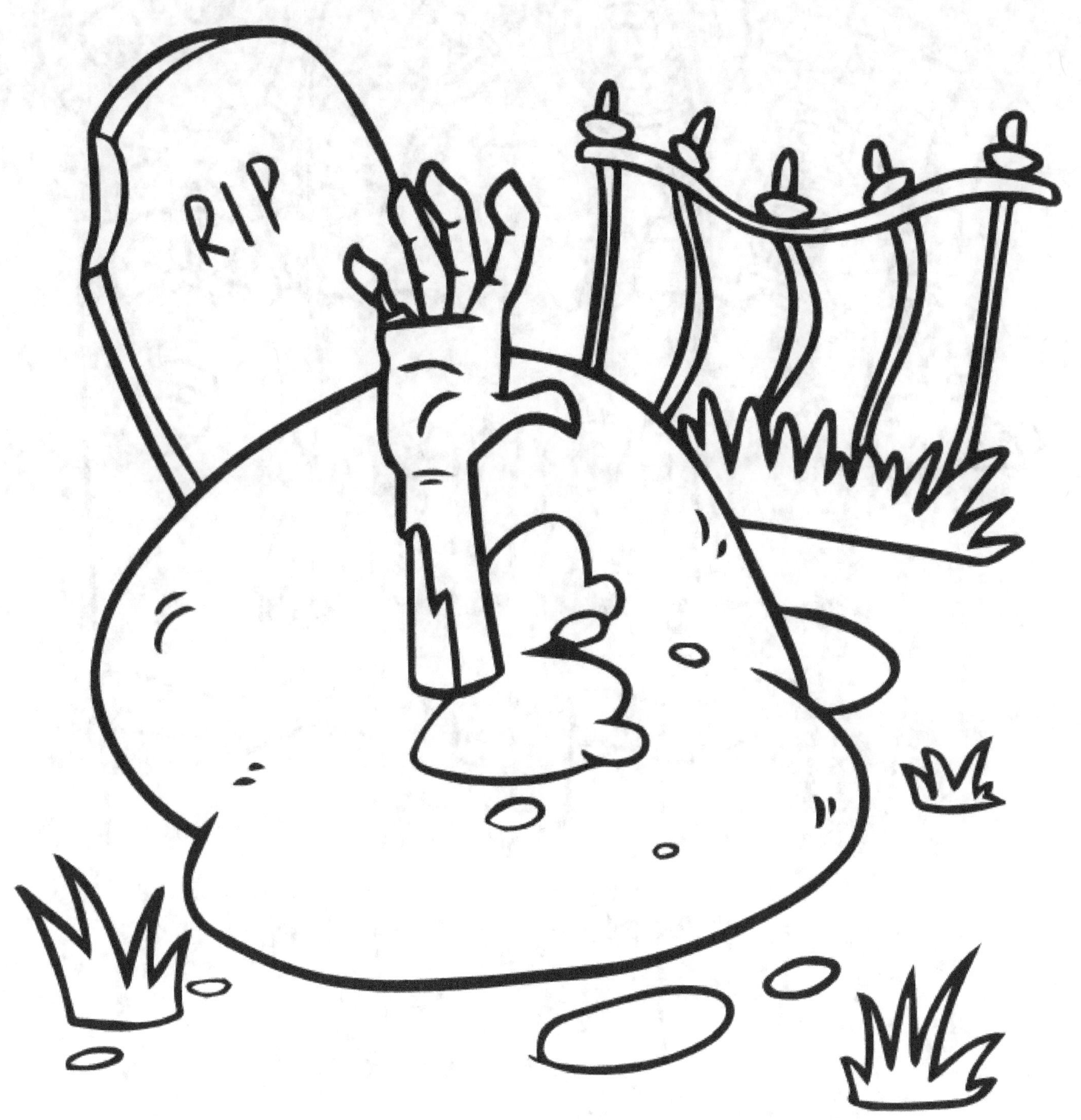

RIP

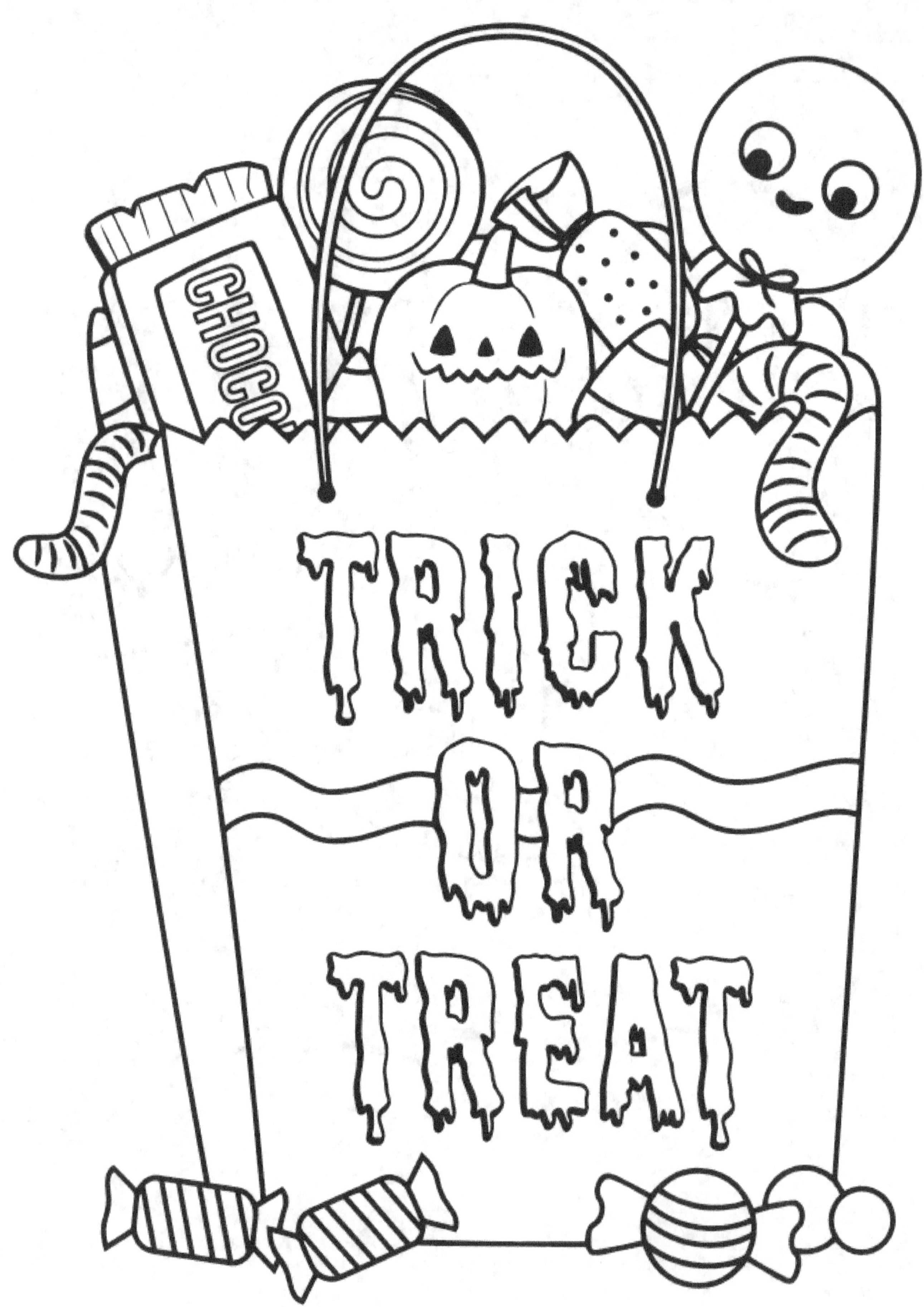

CHOCO
TRICK
OR
TREAT

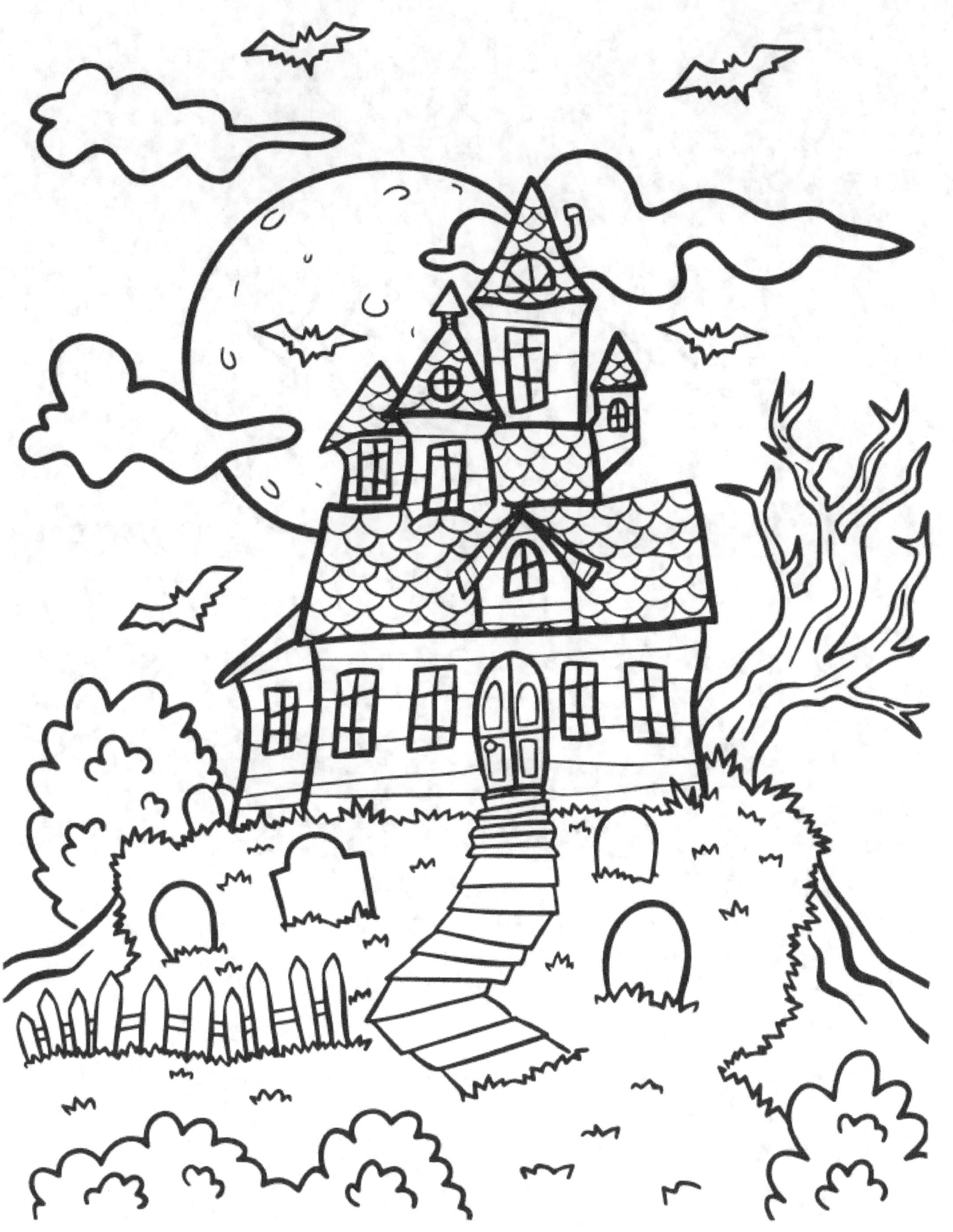

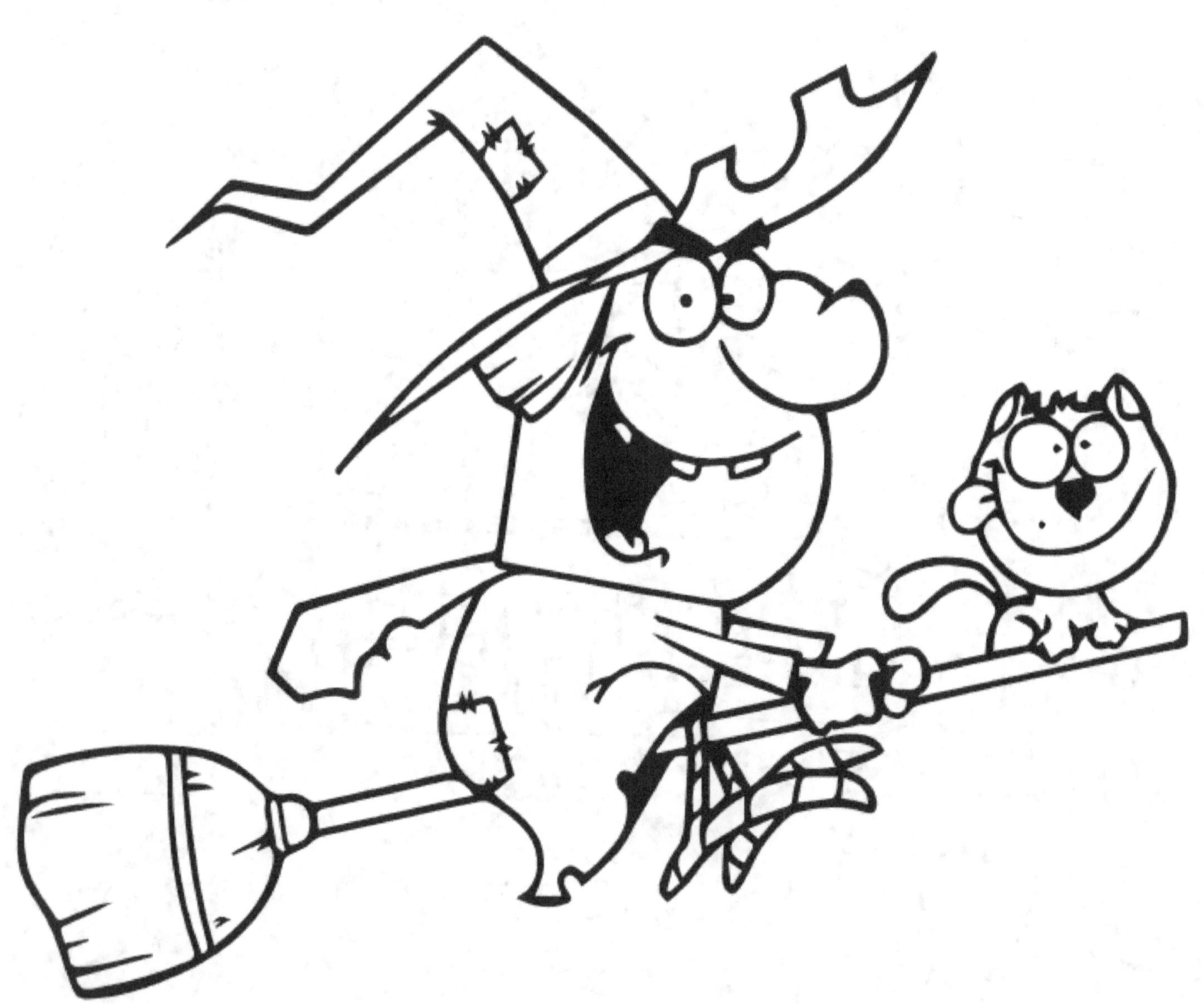

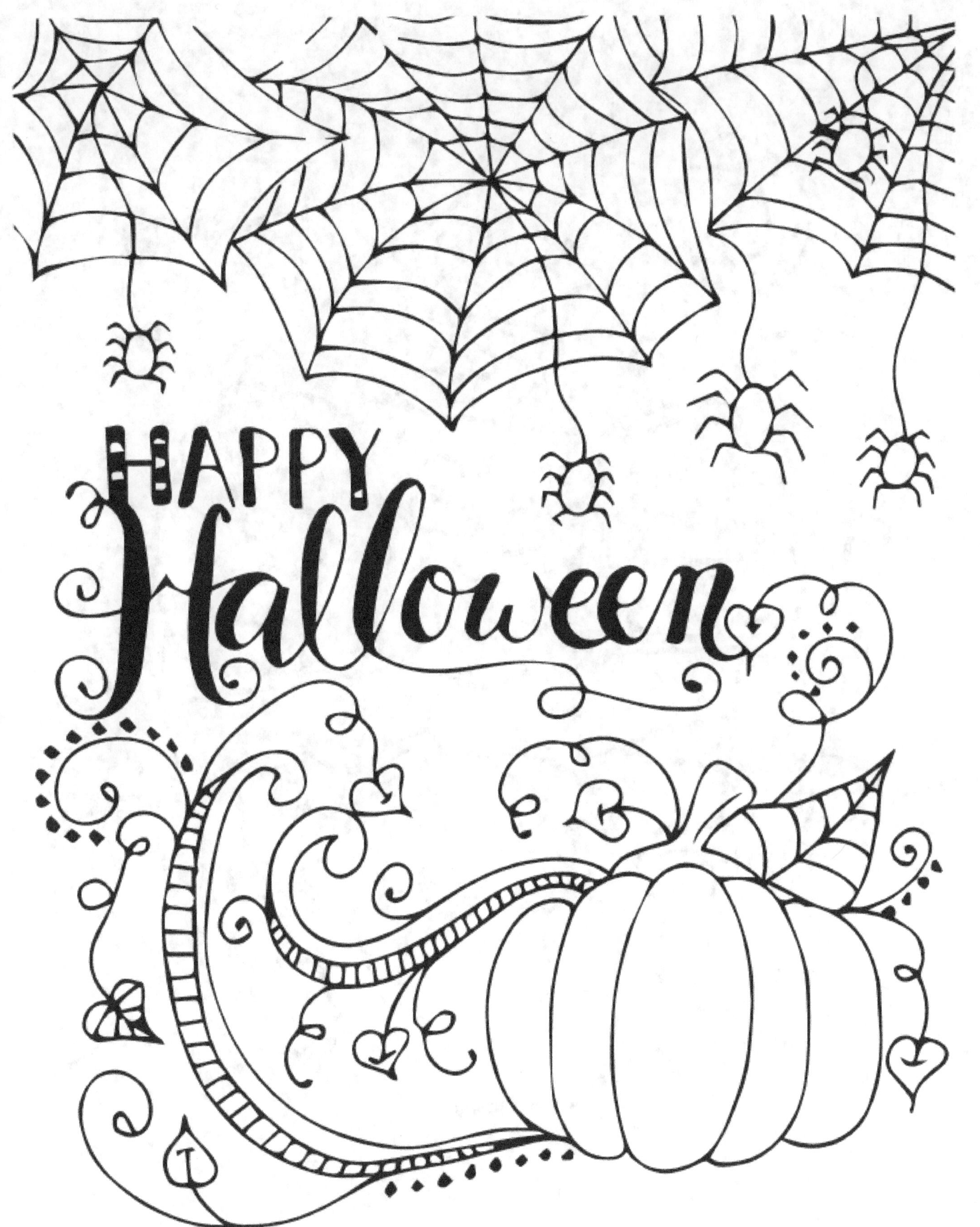
HAPPY
Halloween

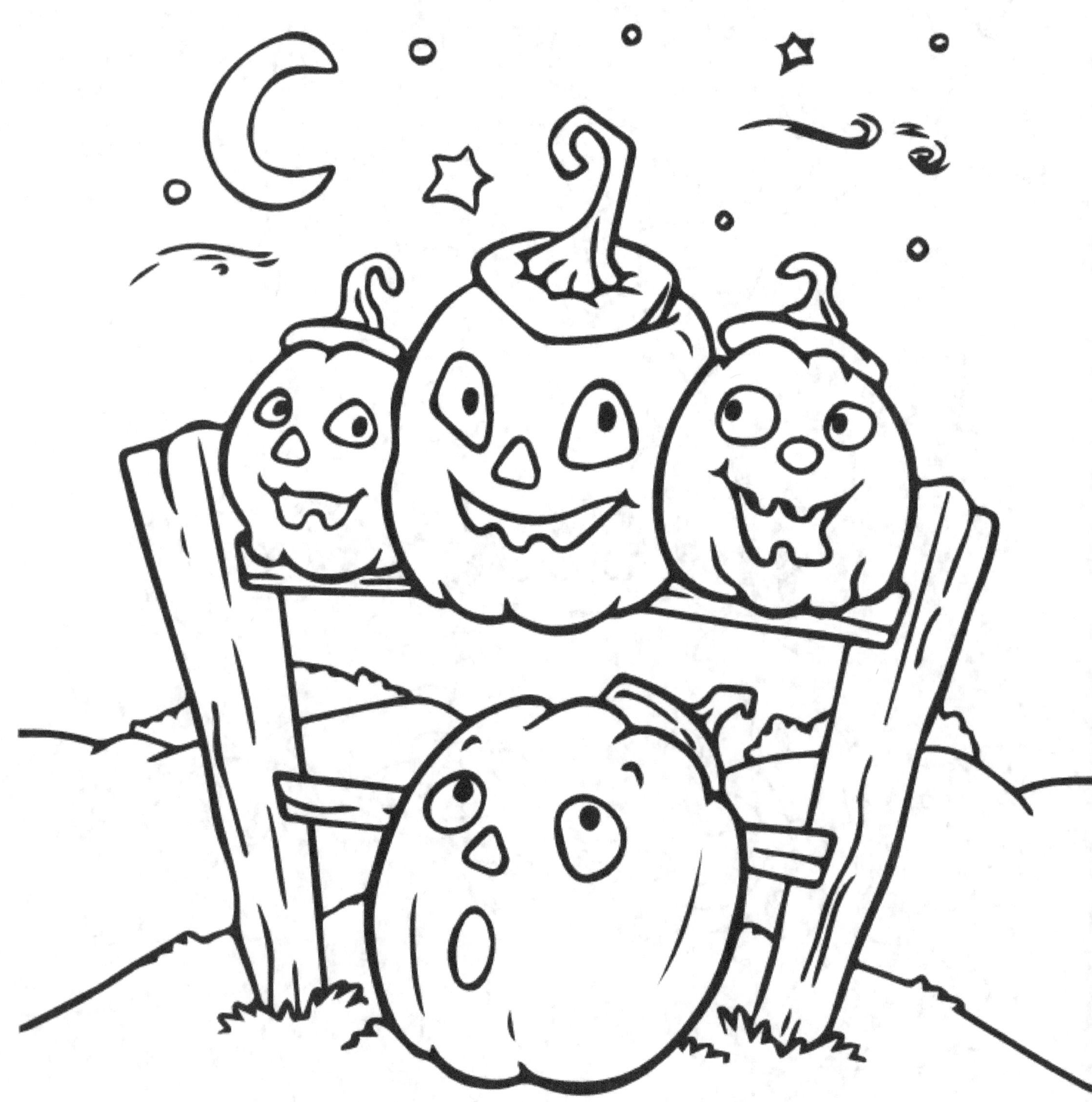

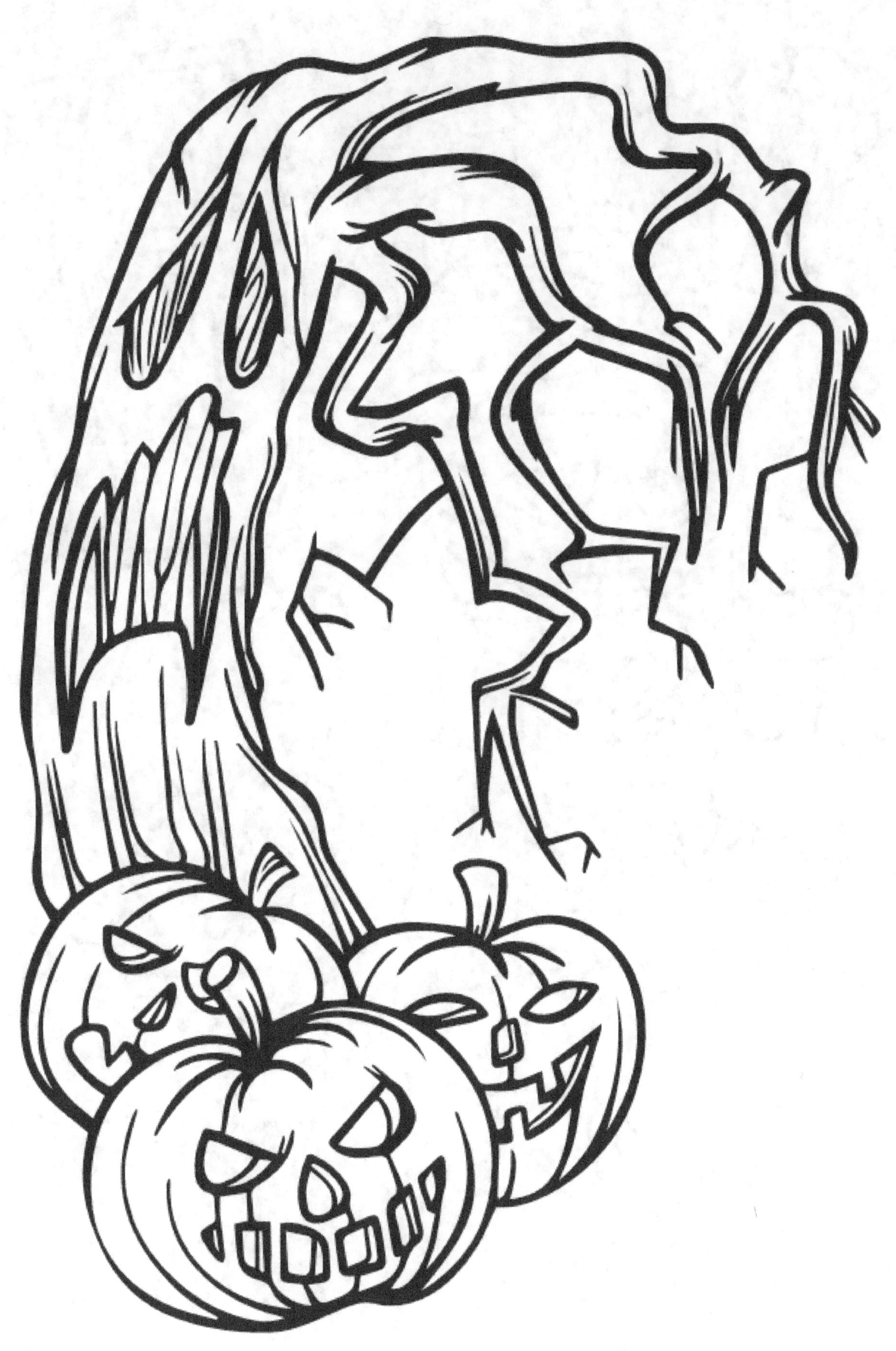

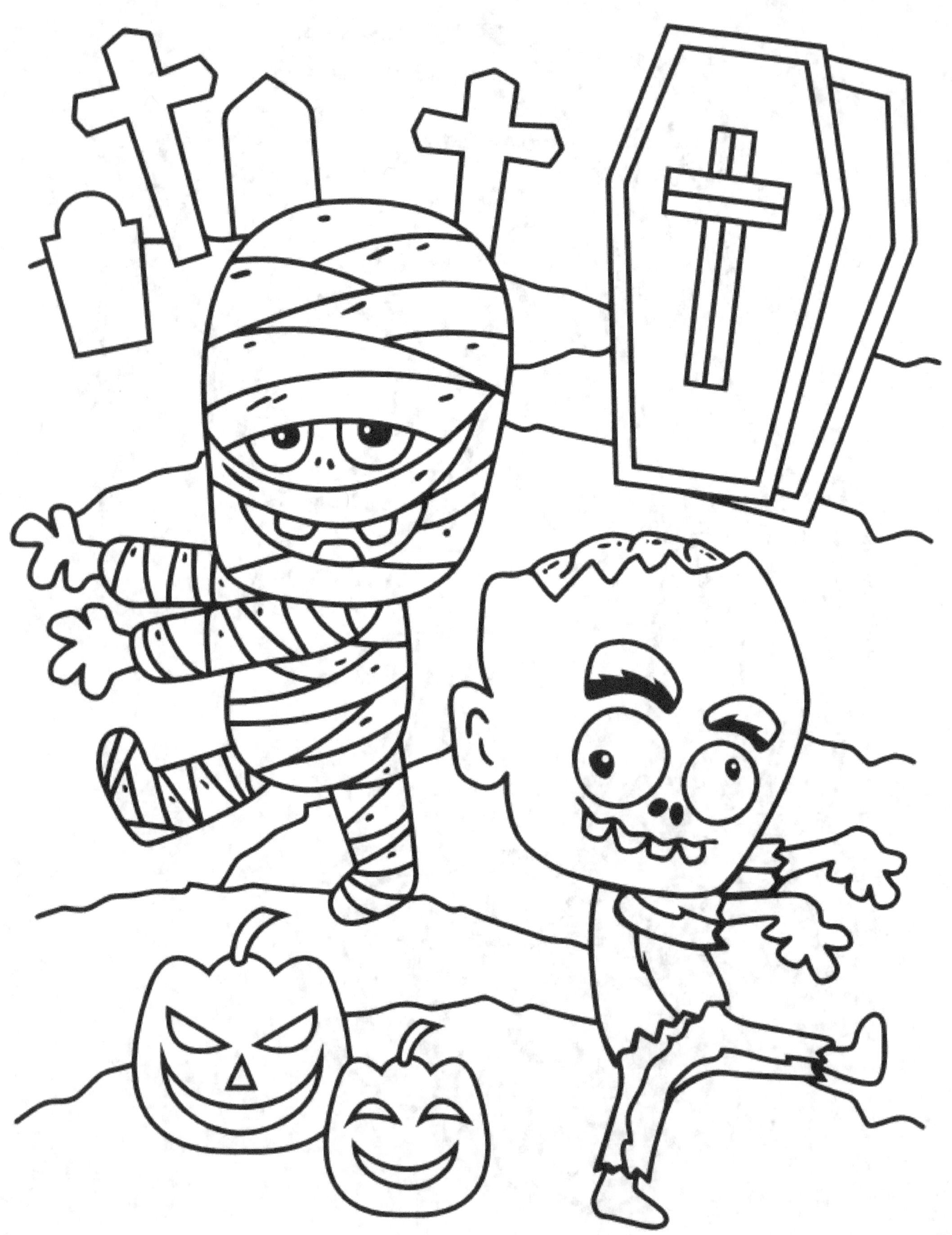

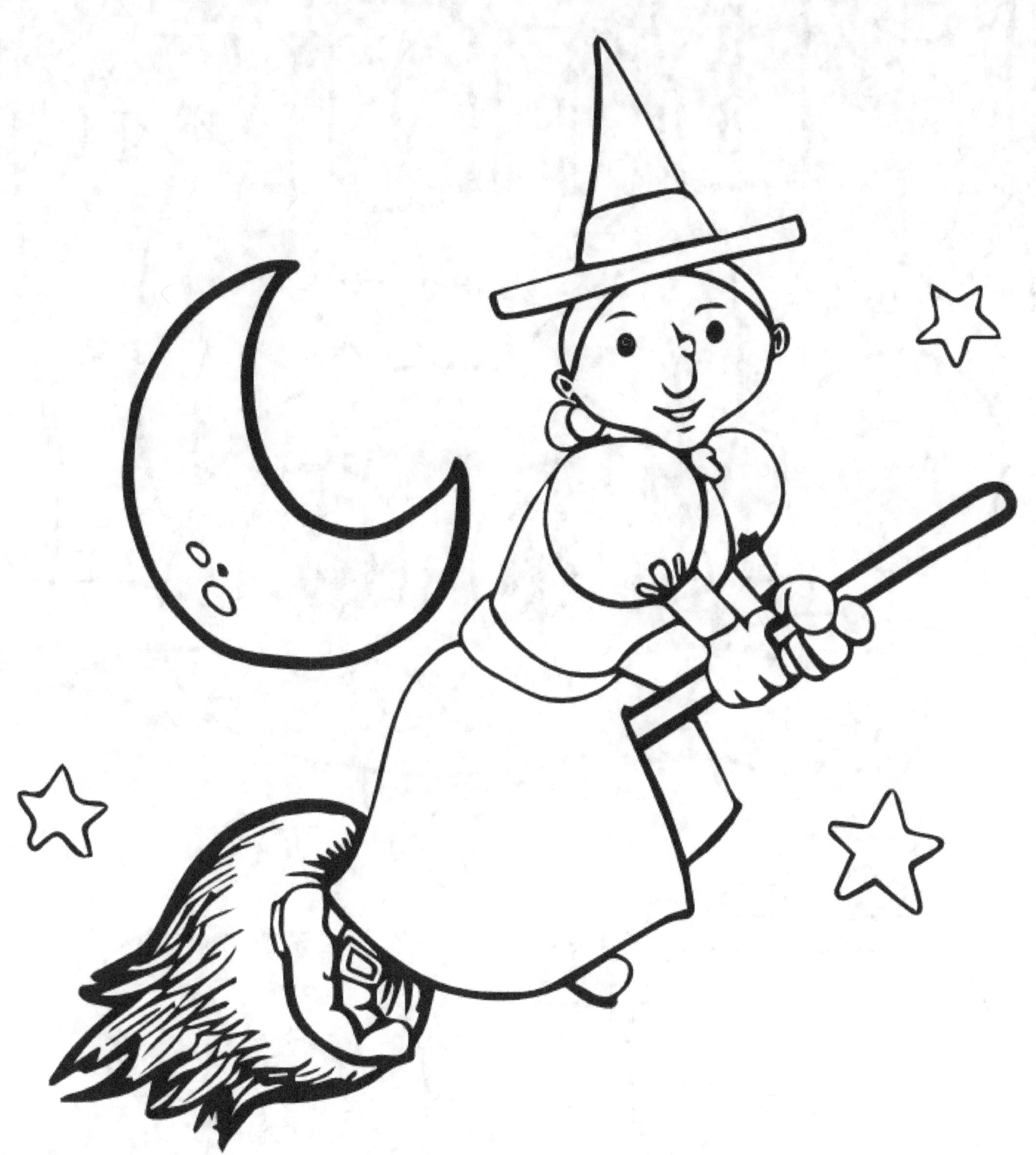

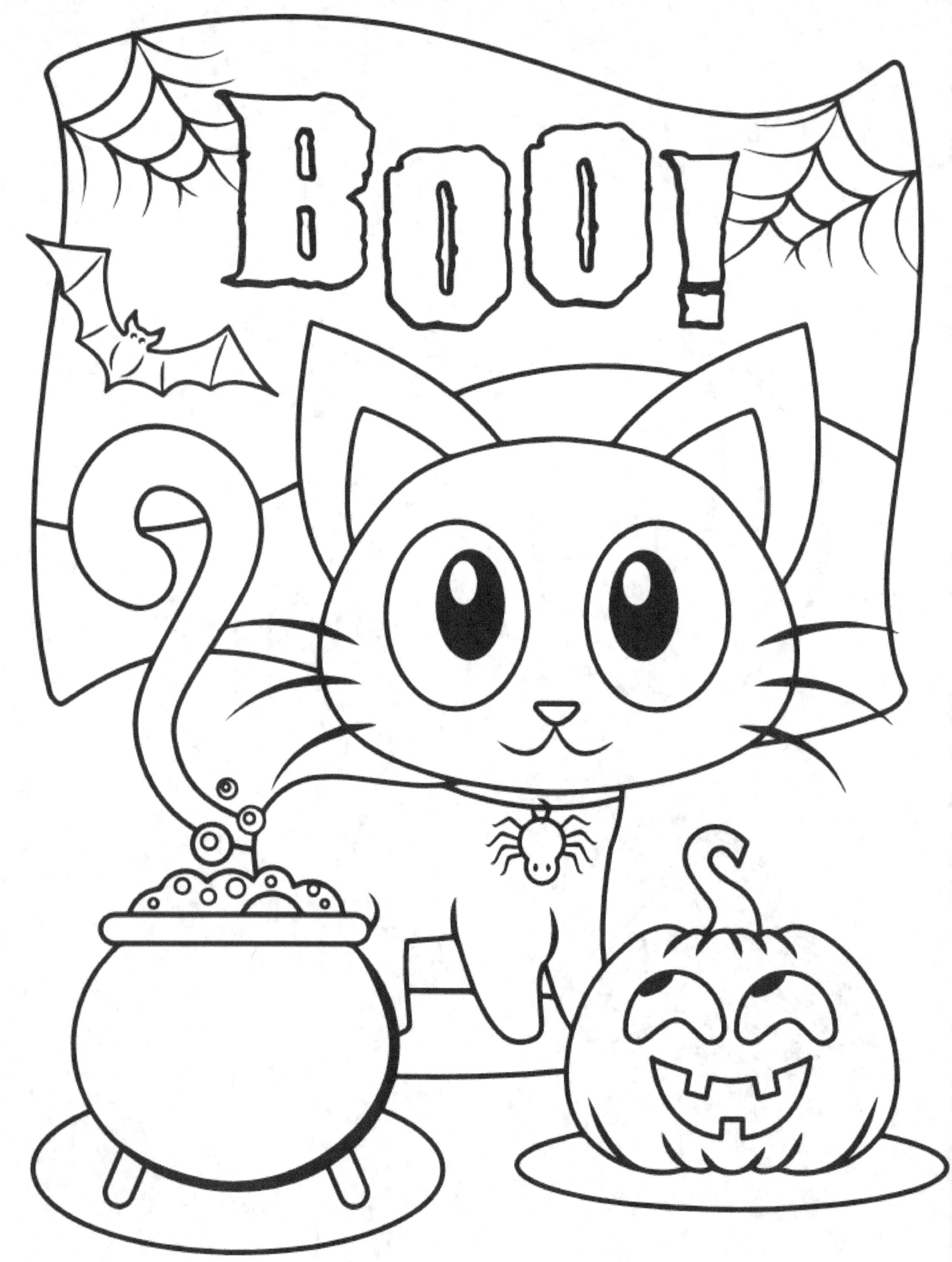
BOO!

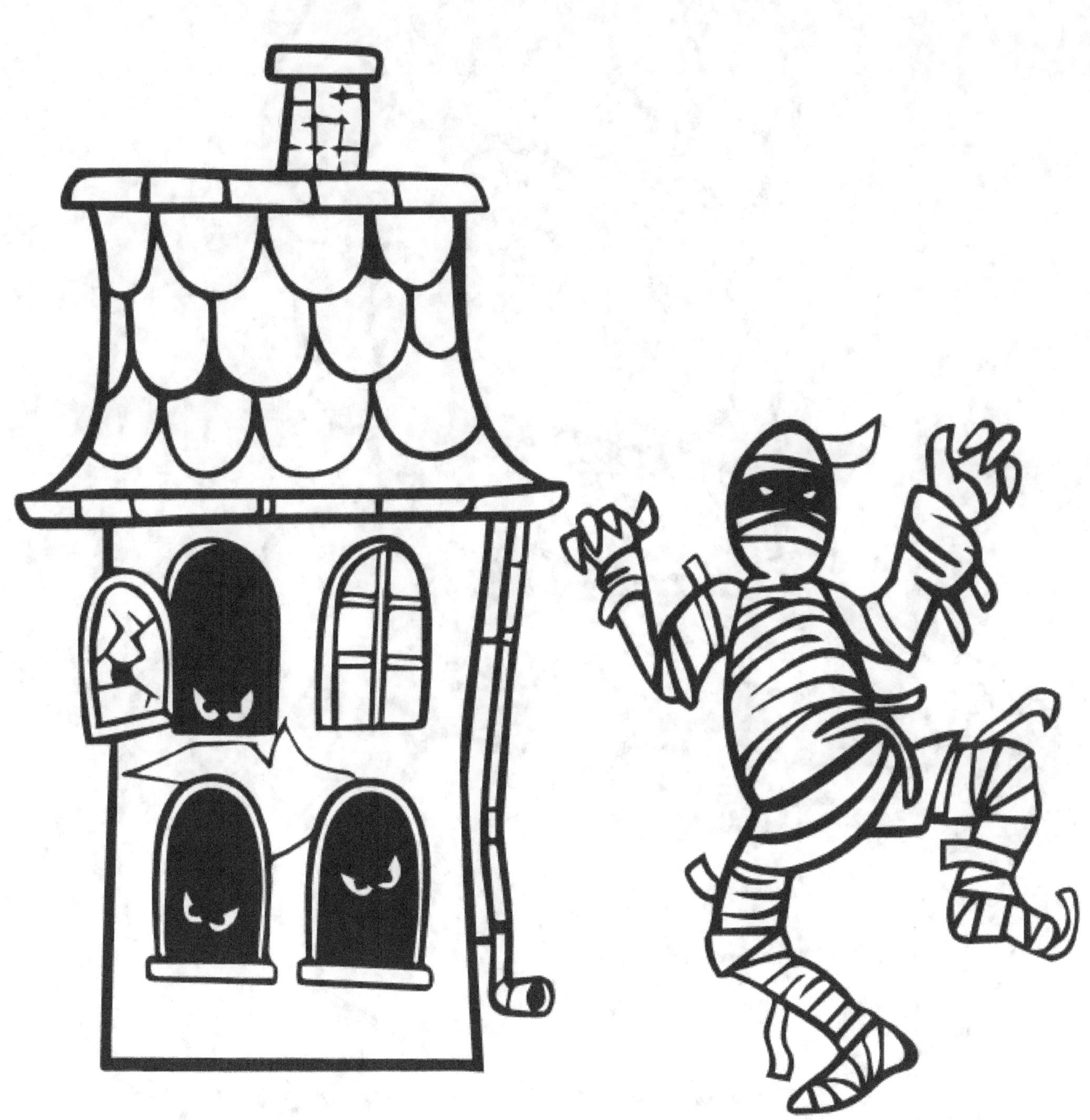

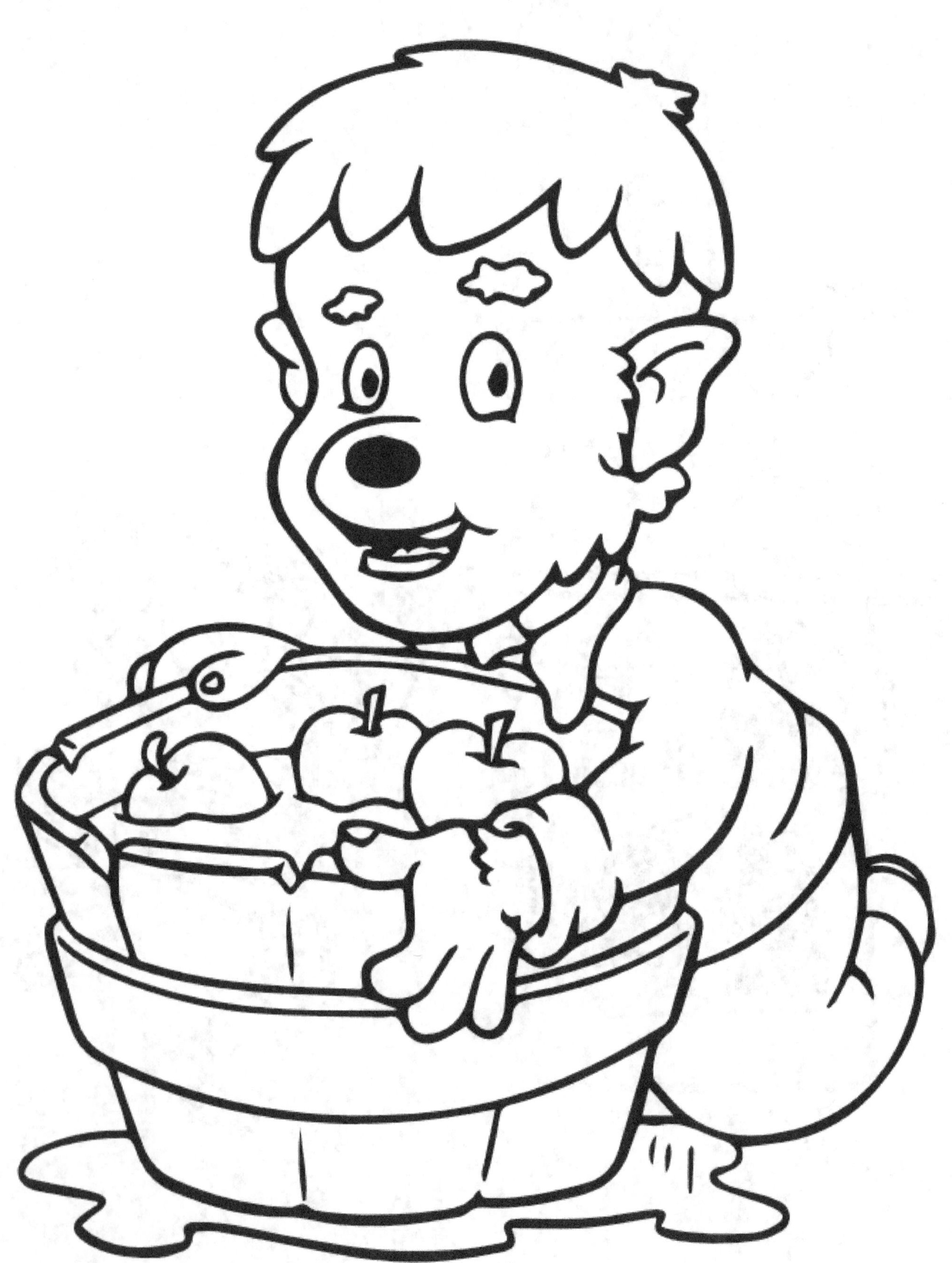

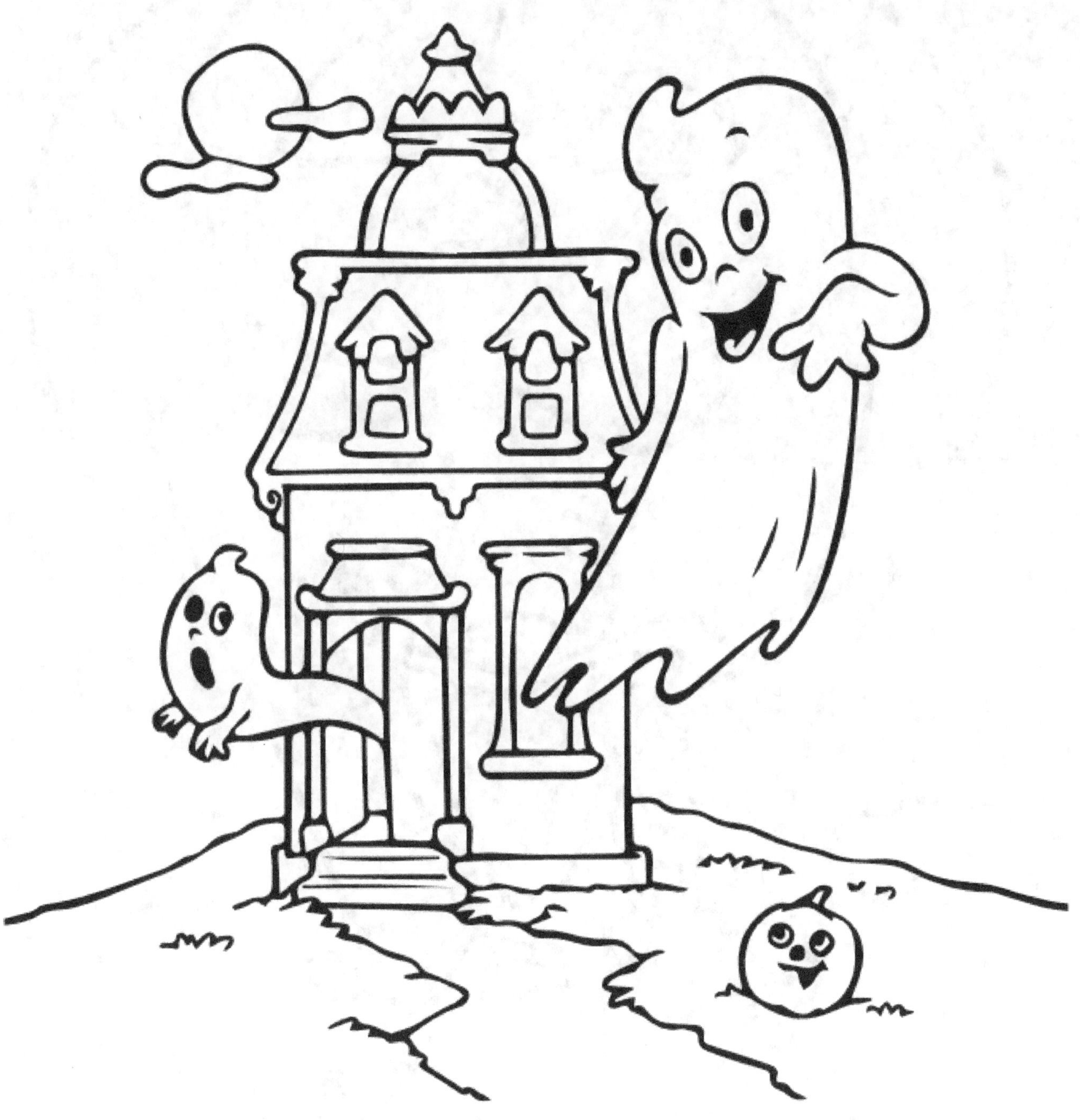

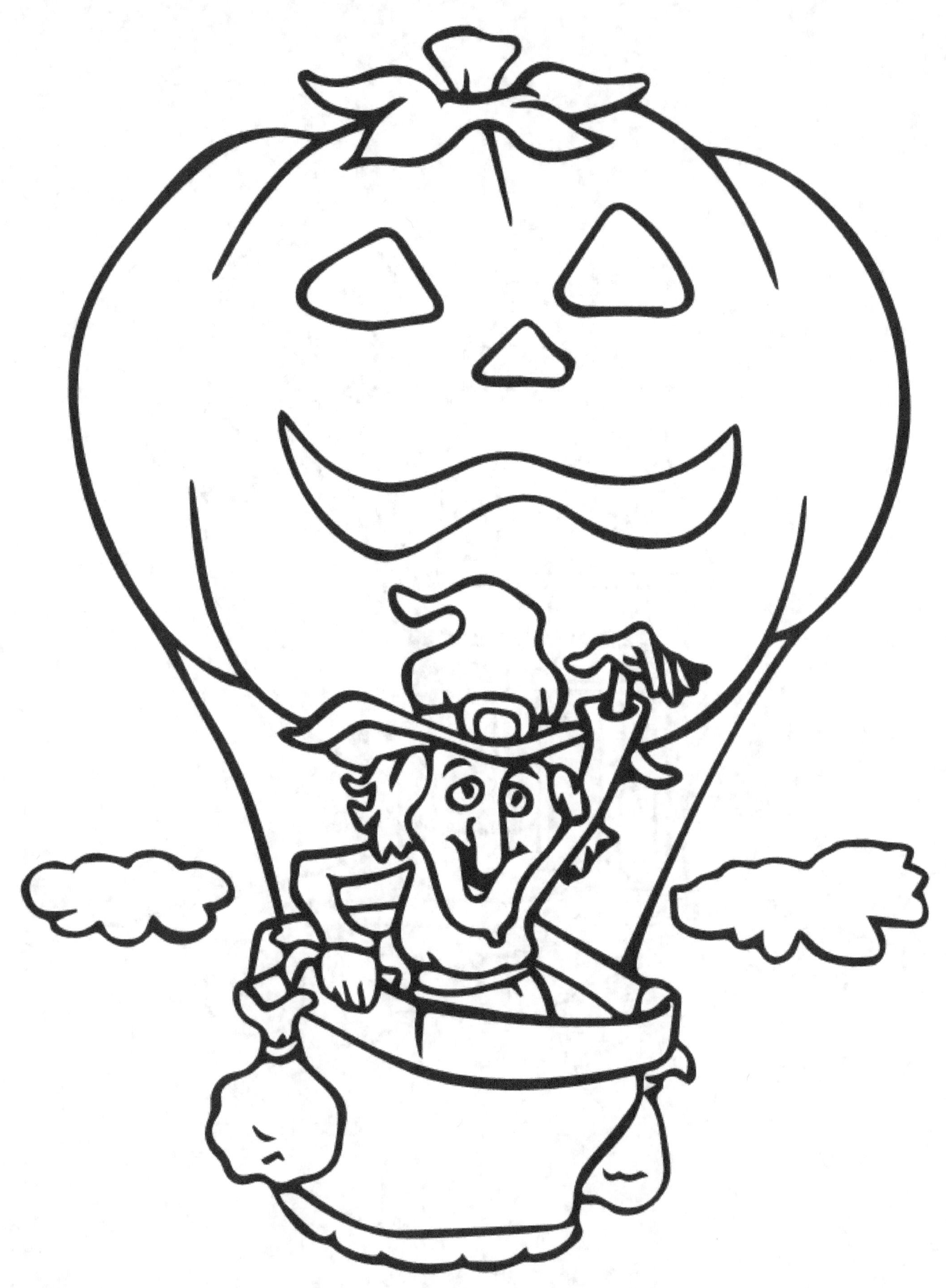

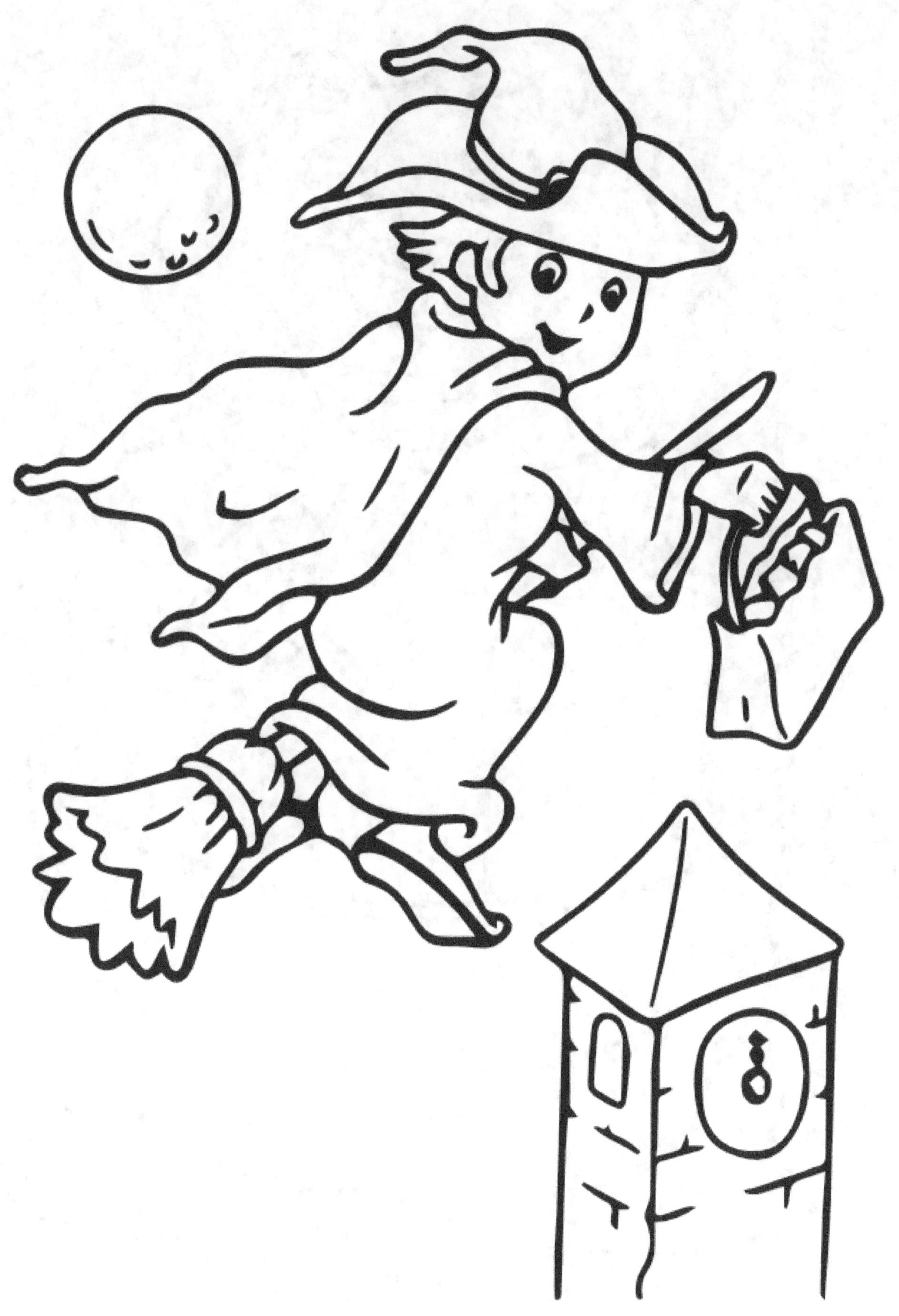

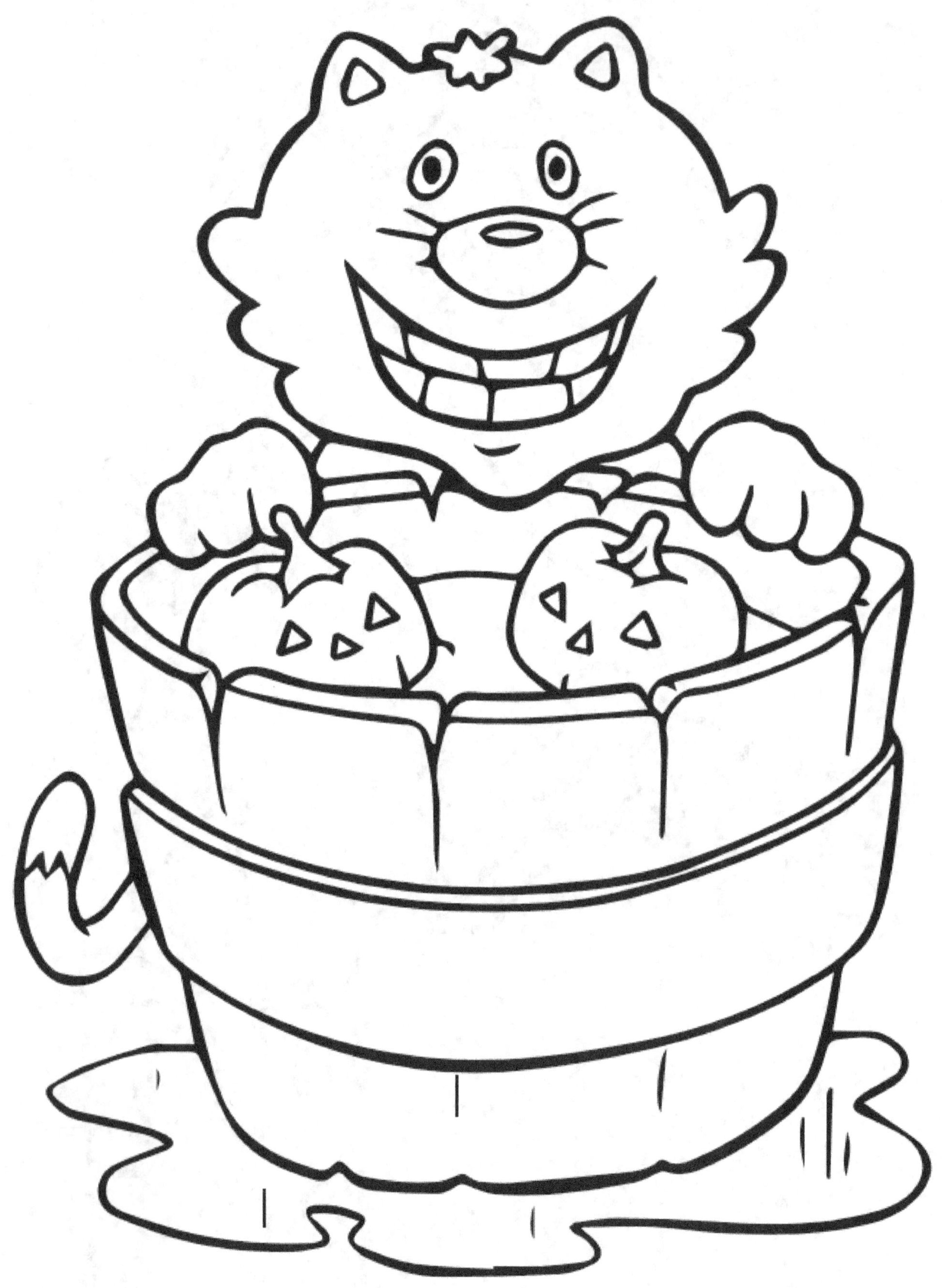

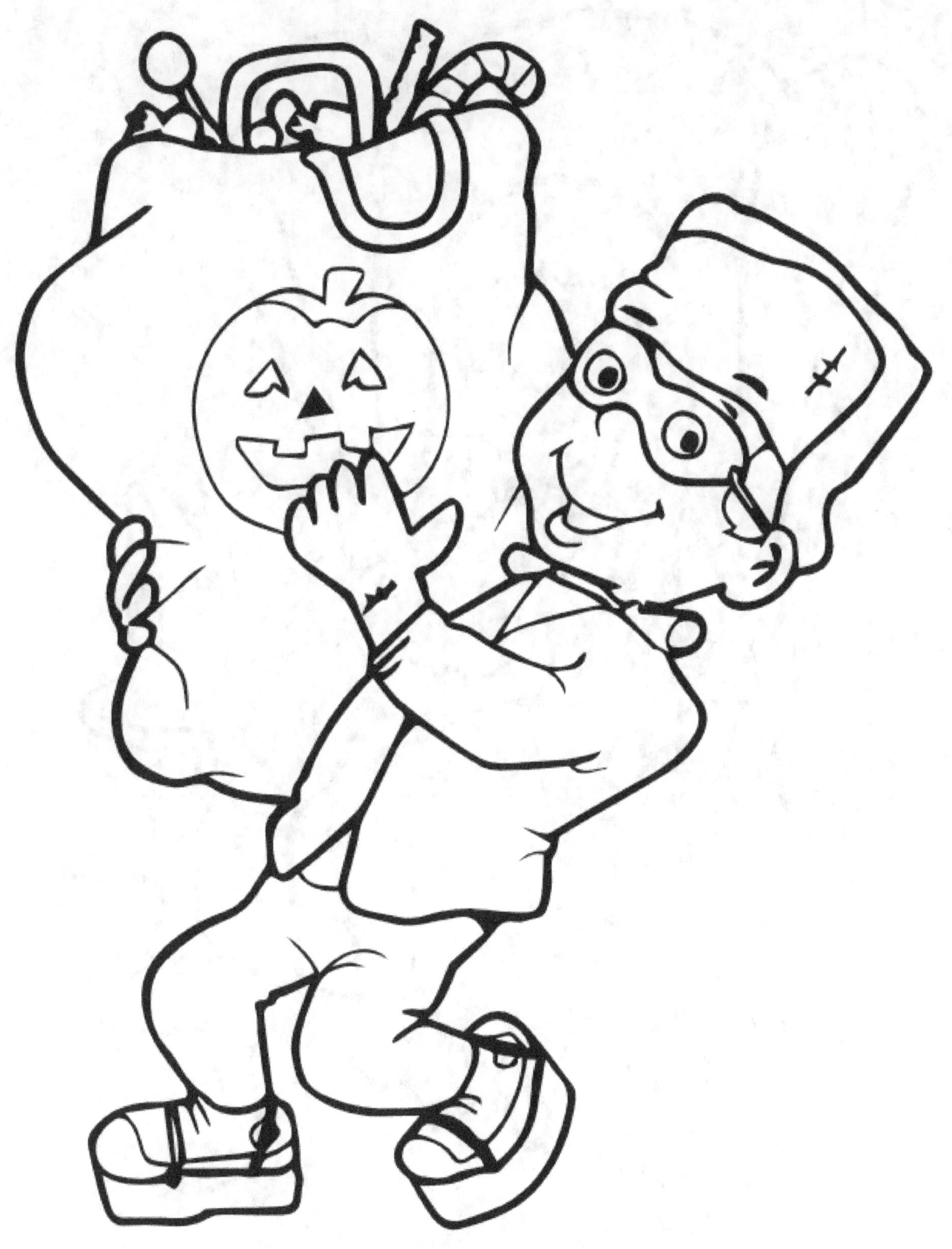

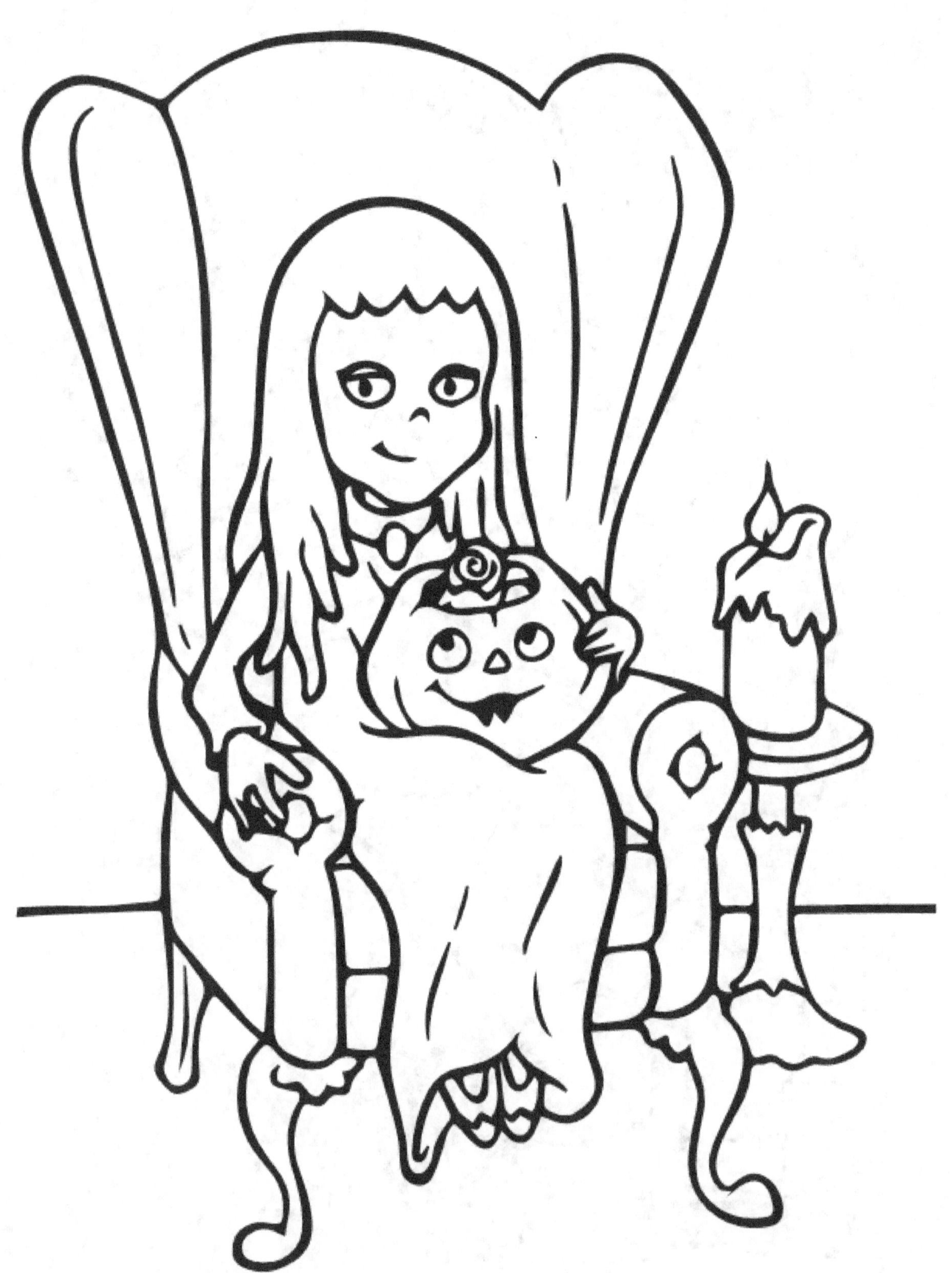

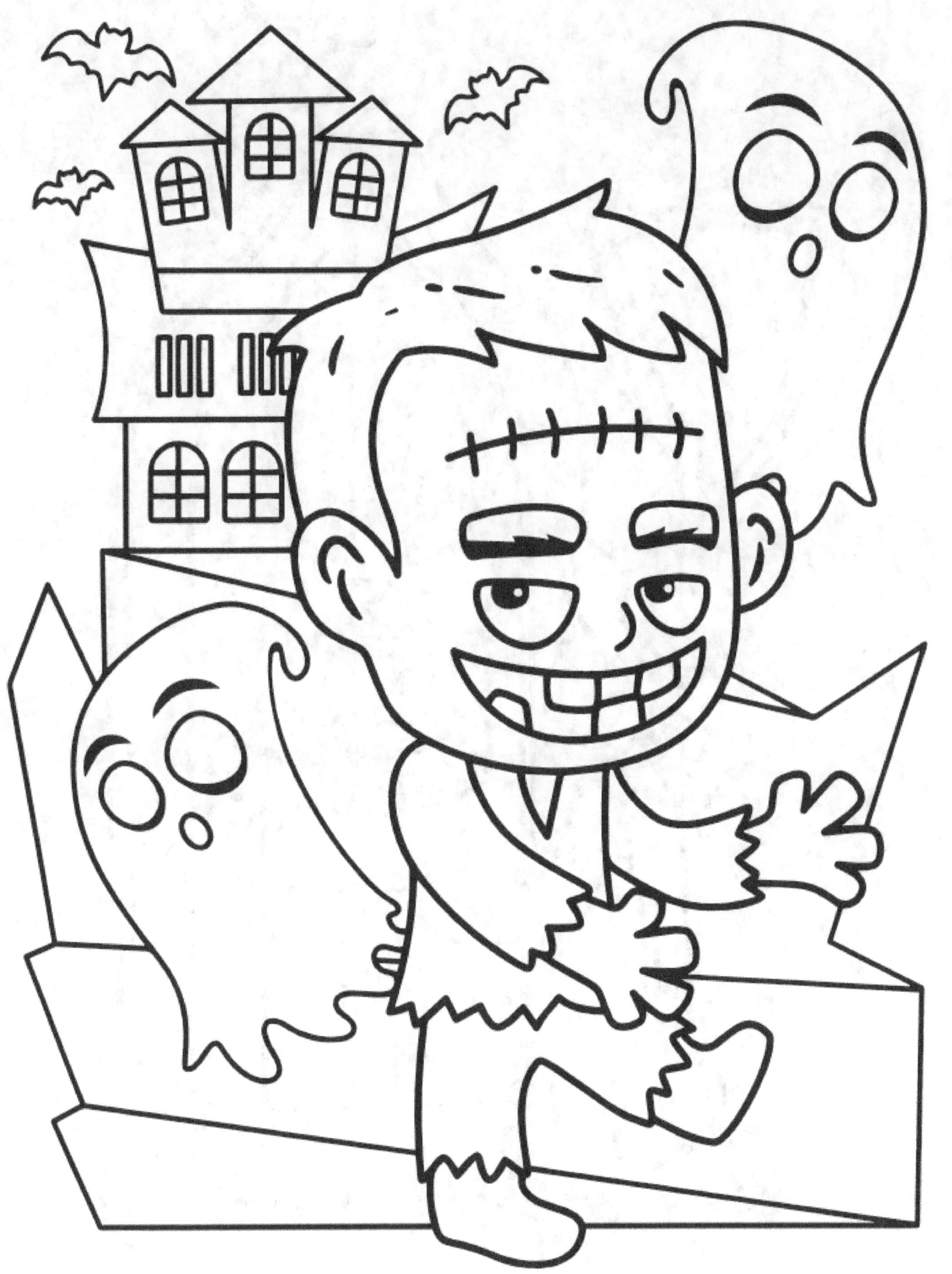

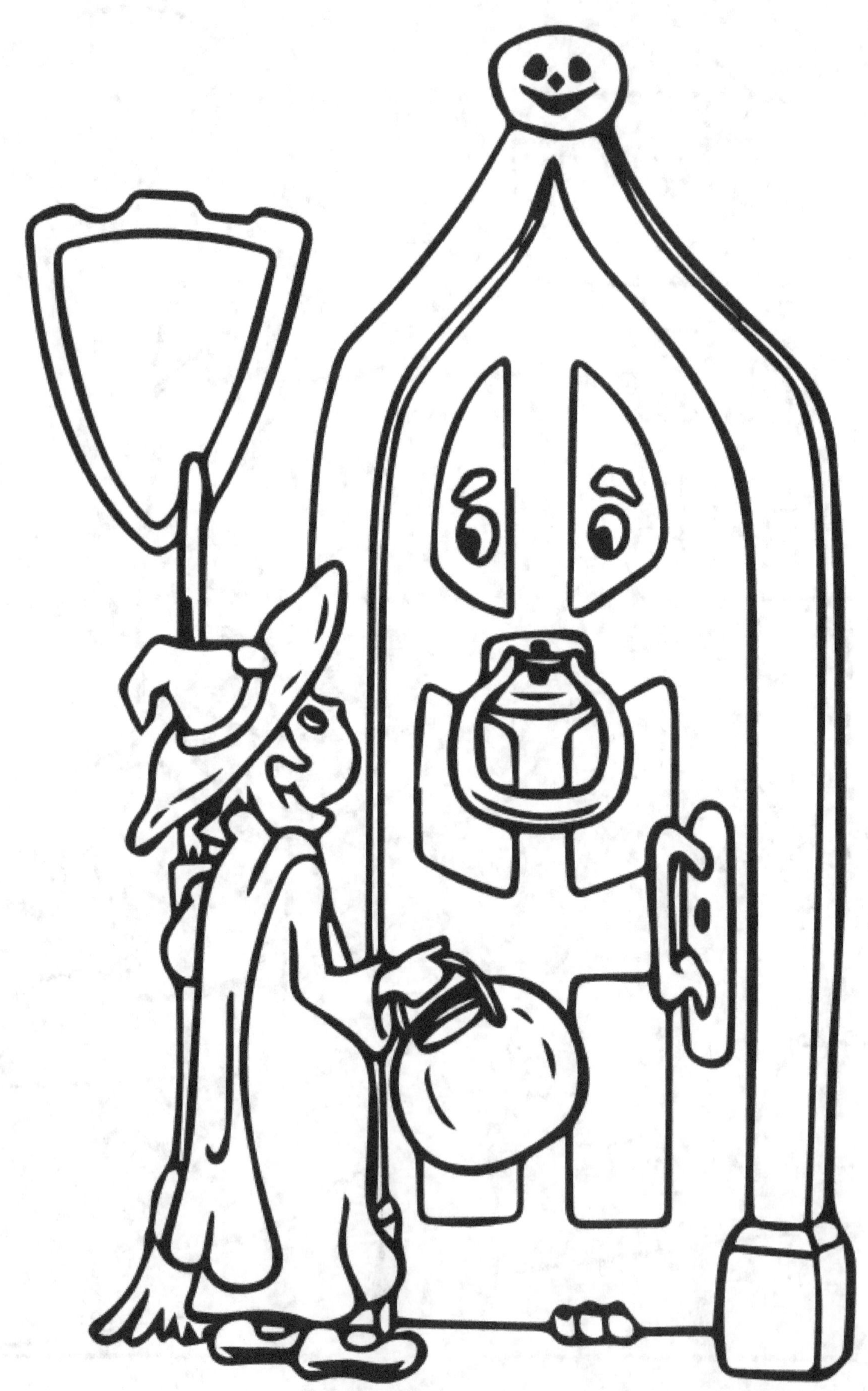

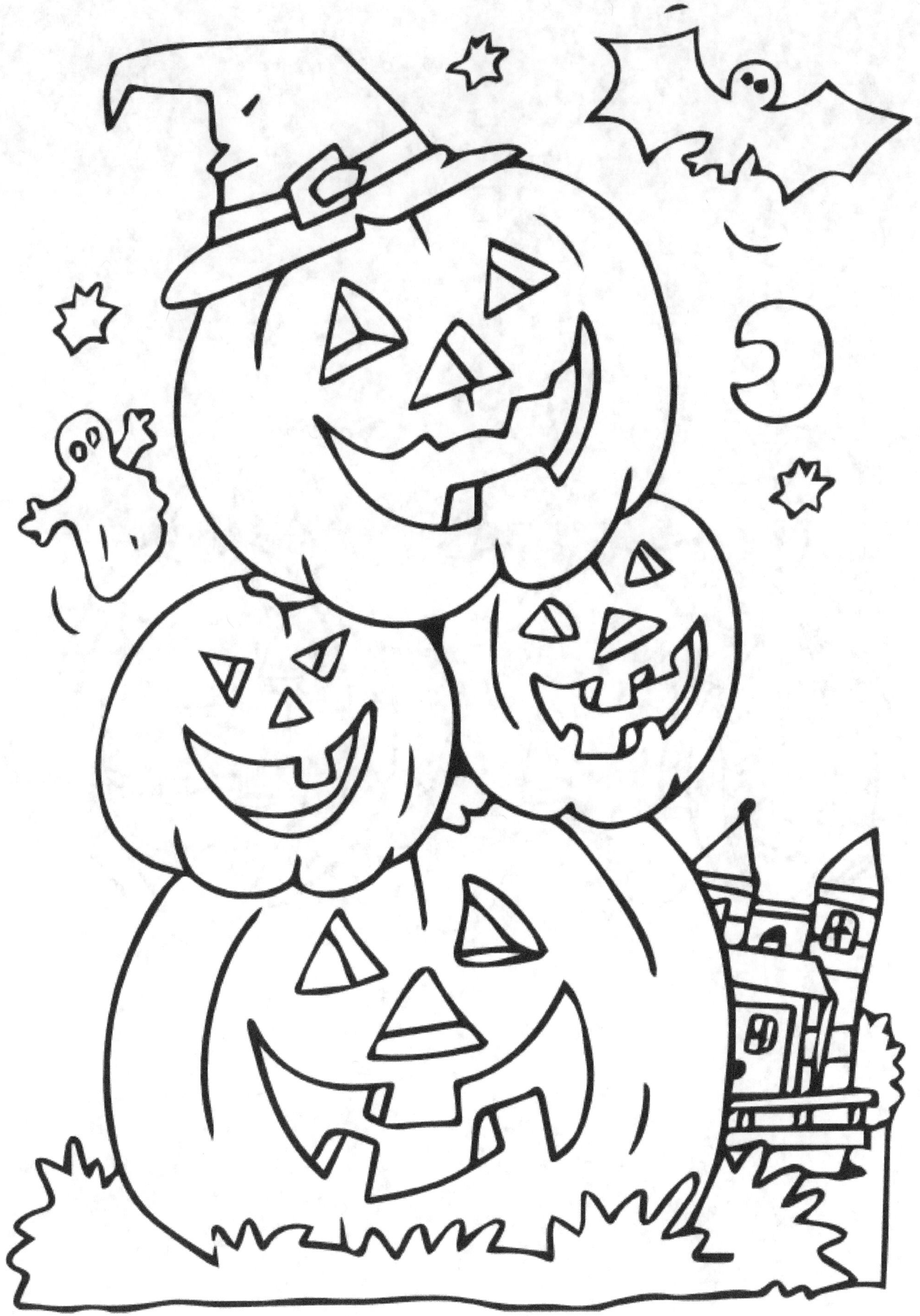

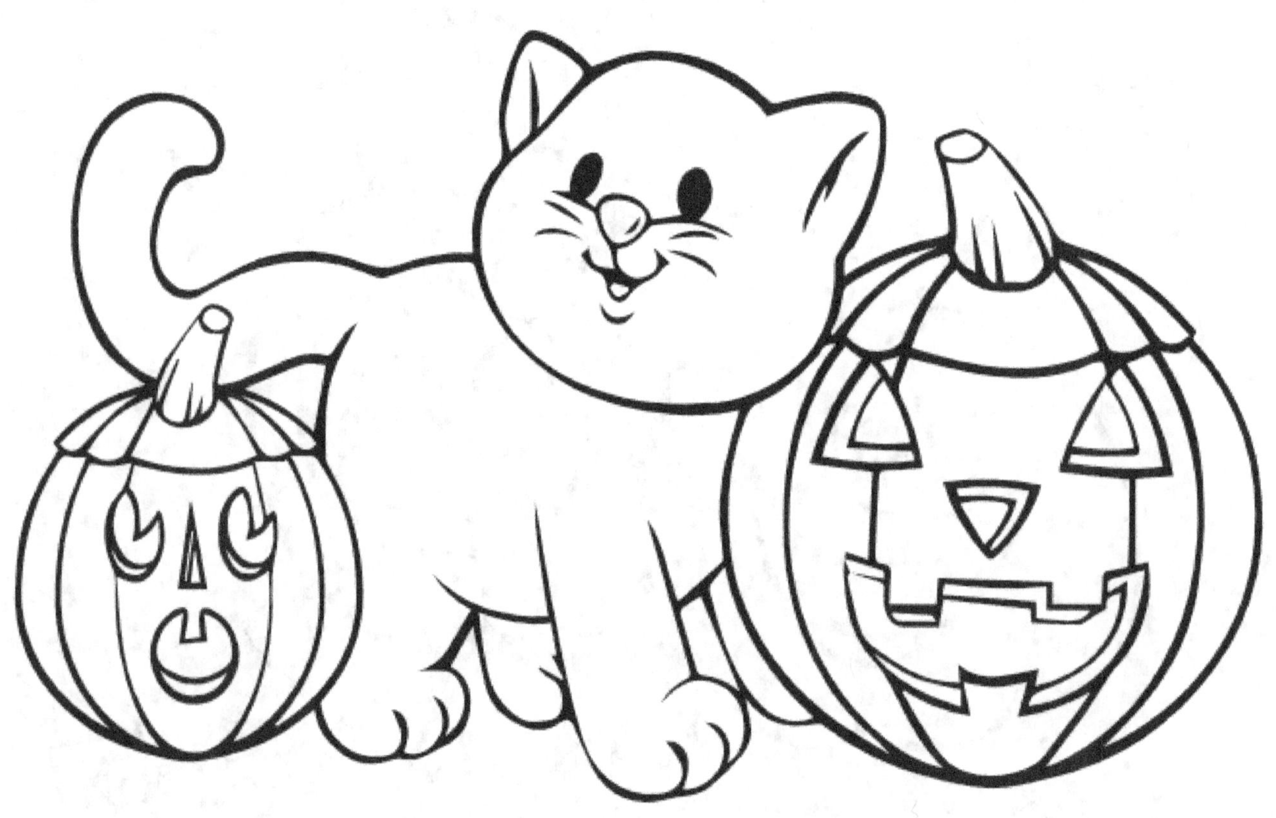

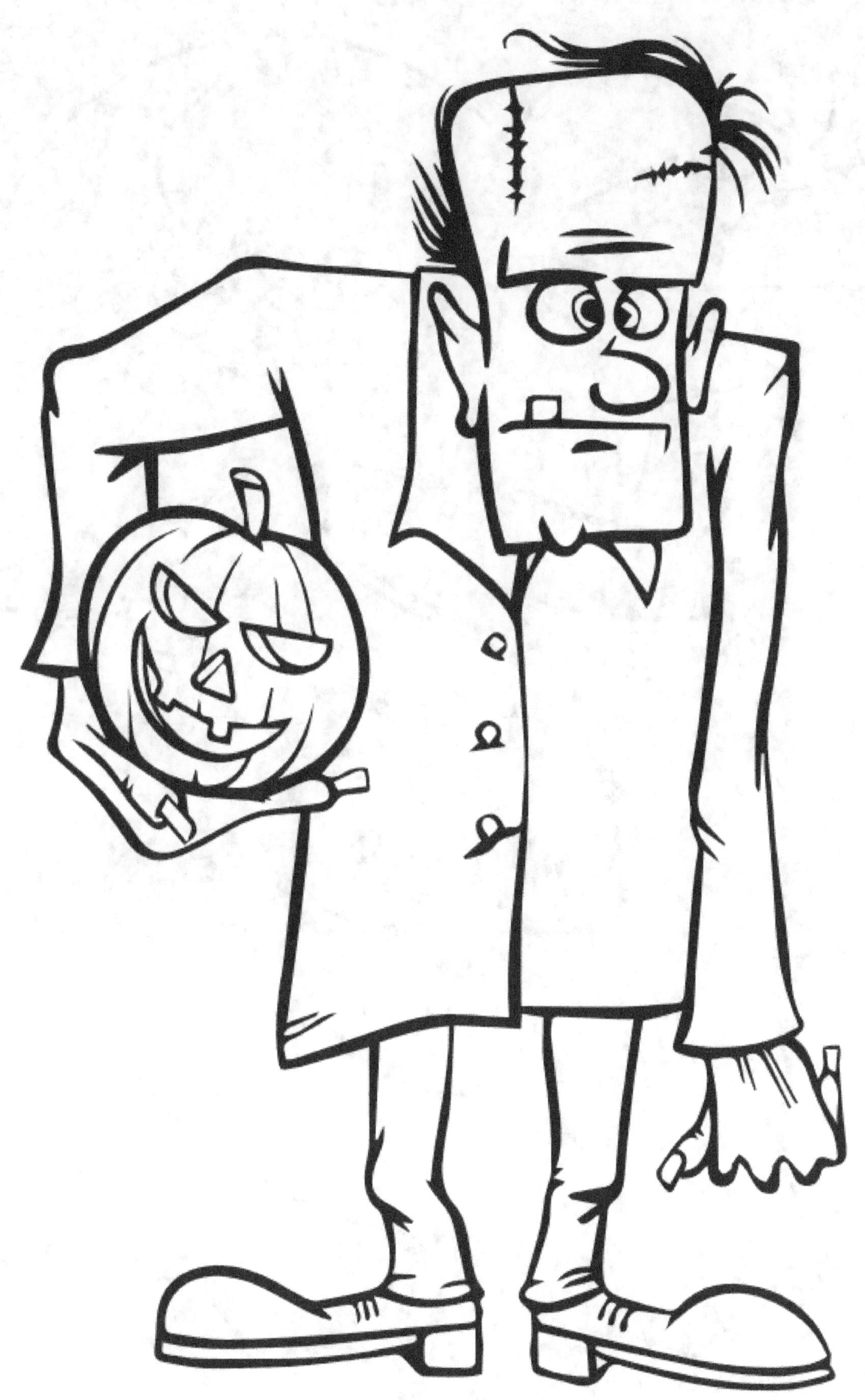

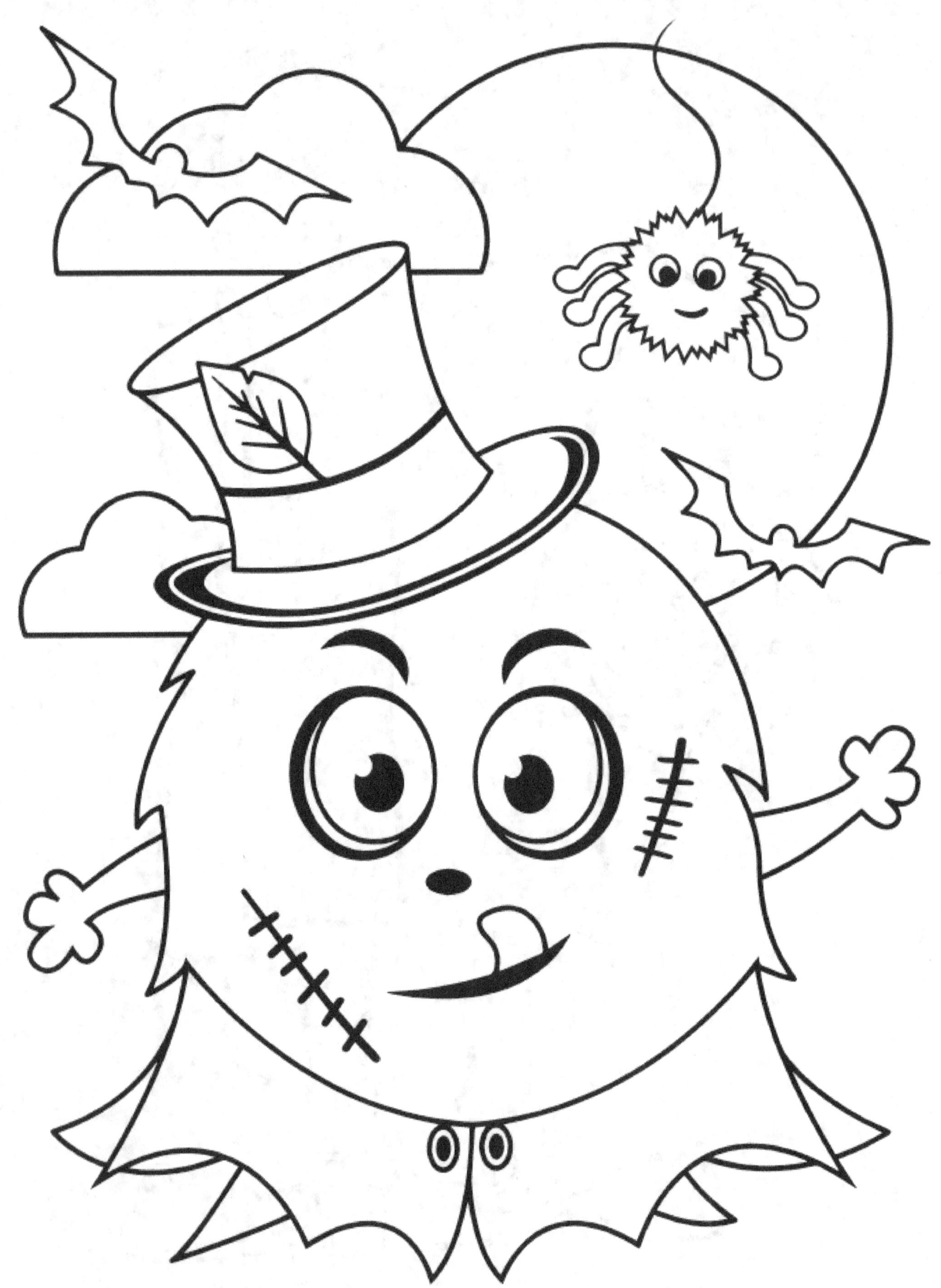

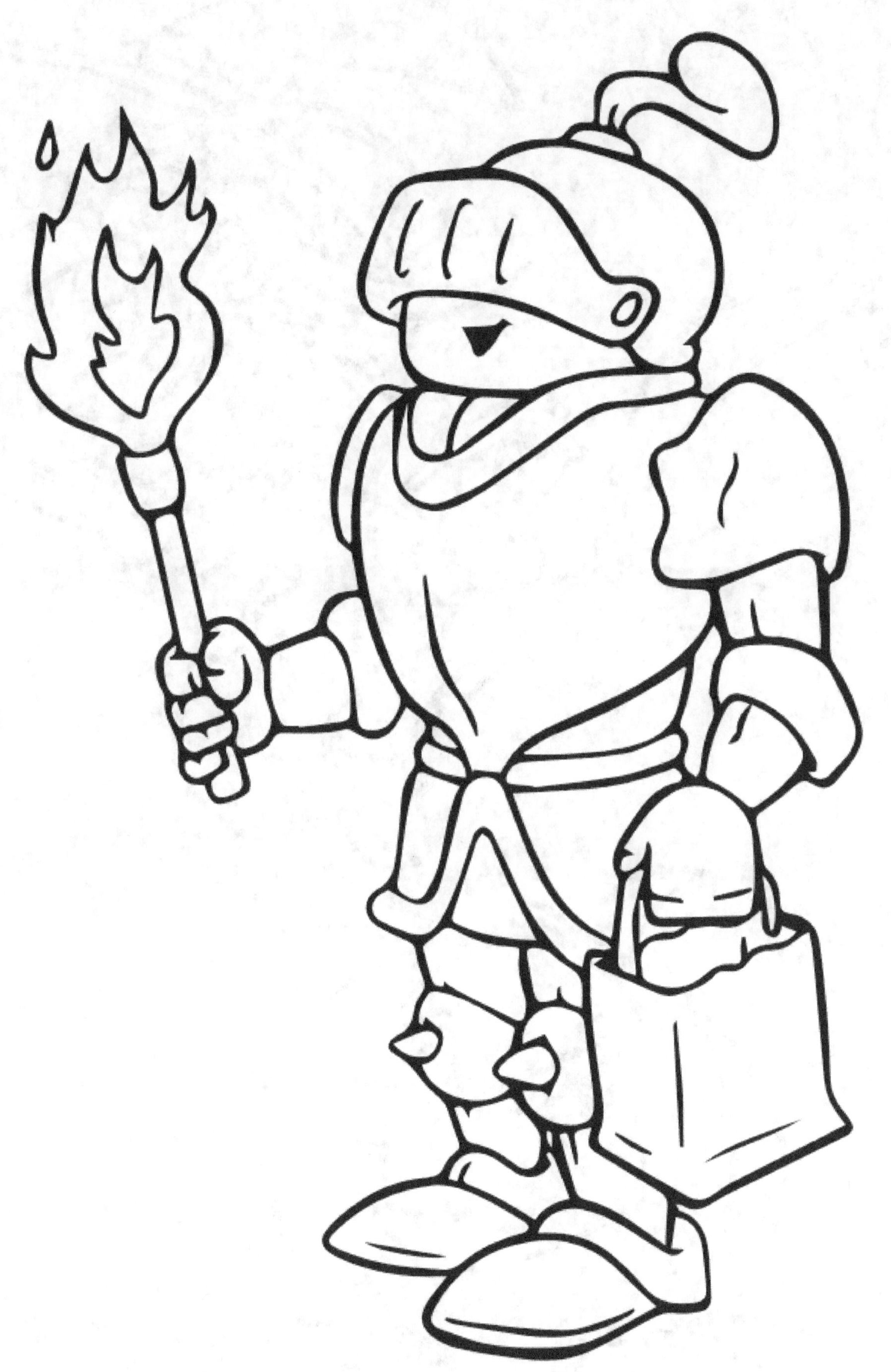

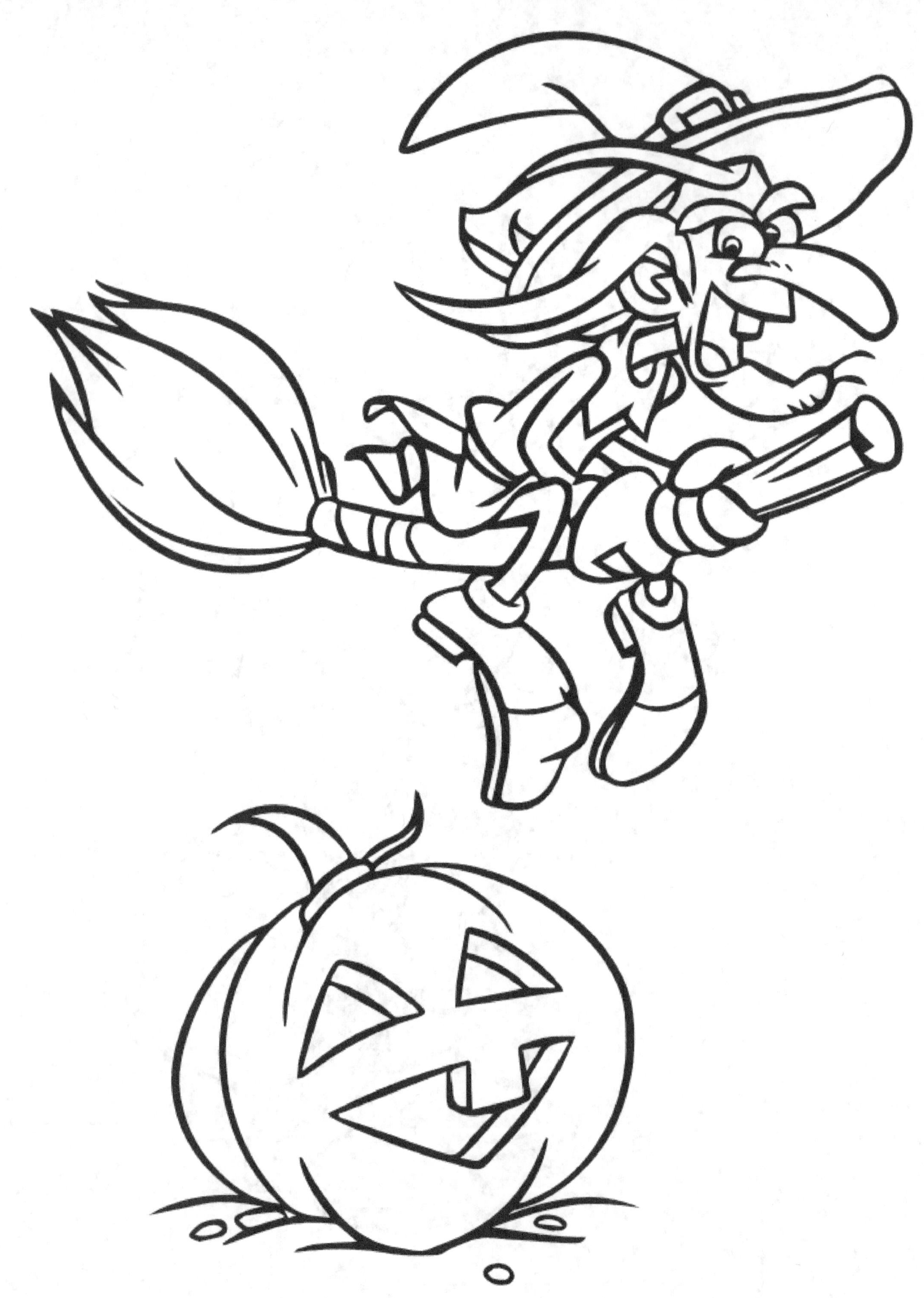

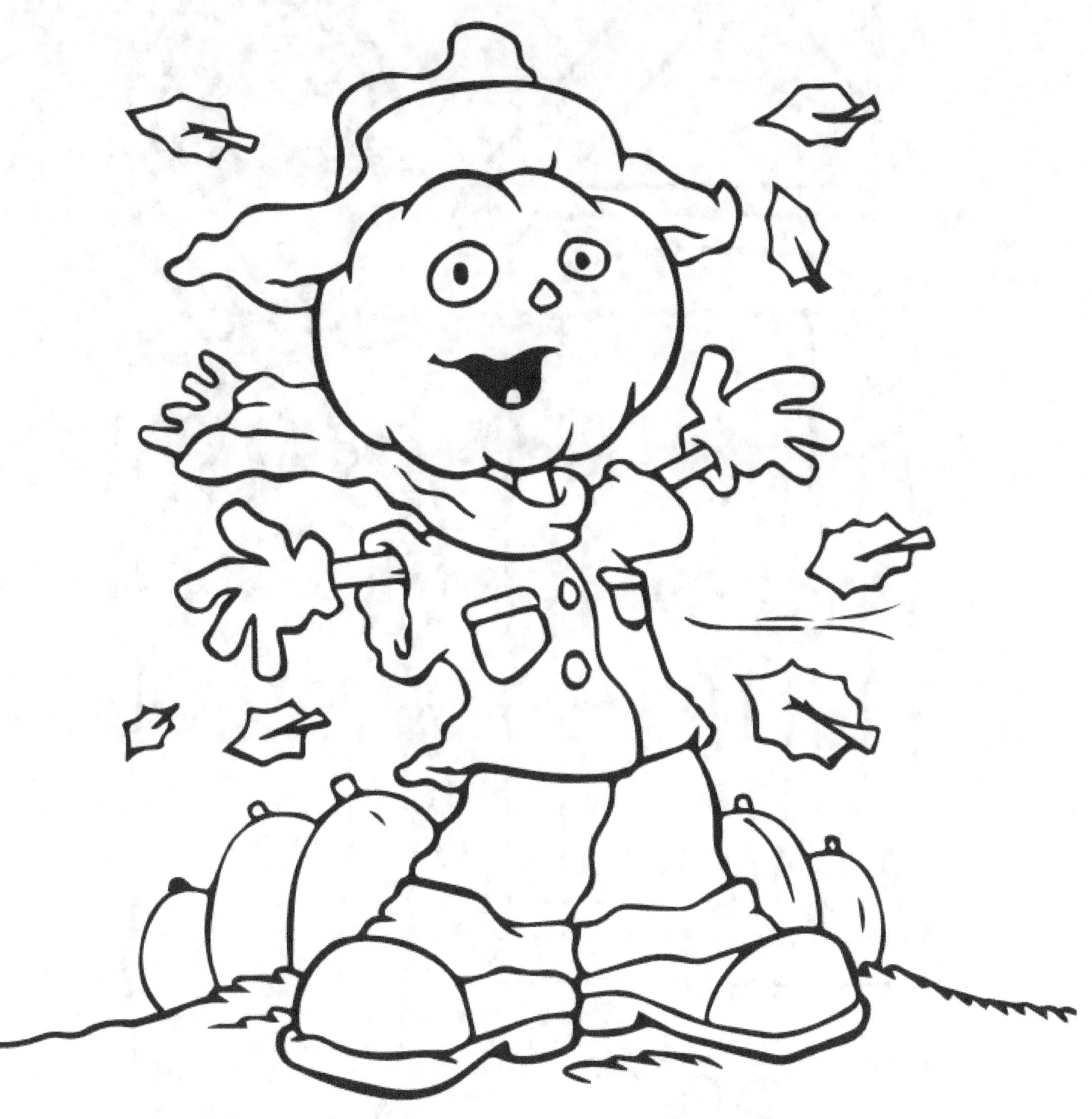

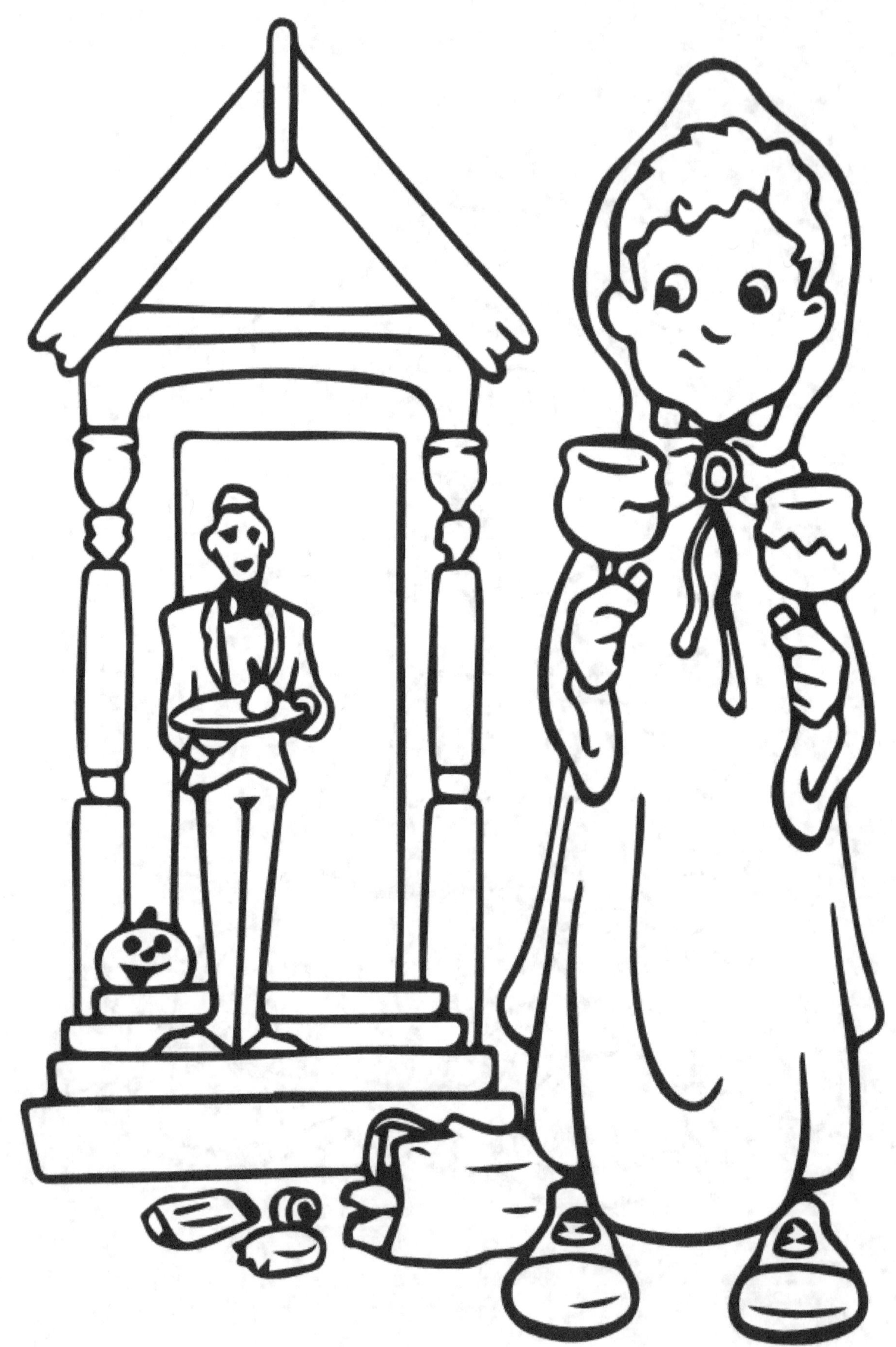

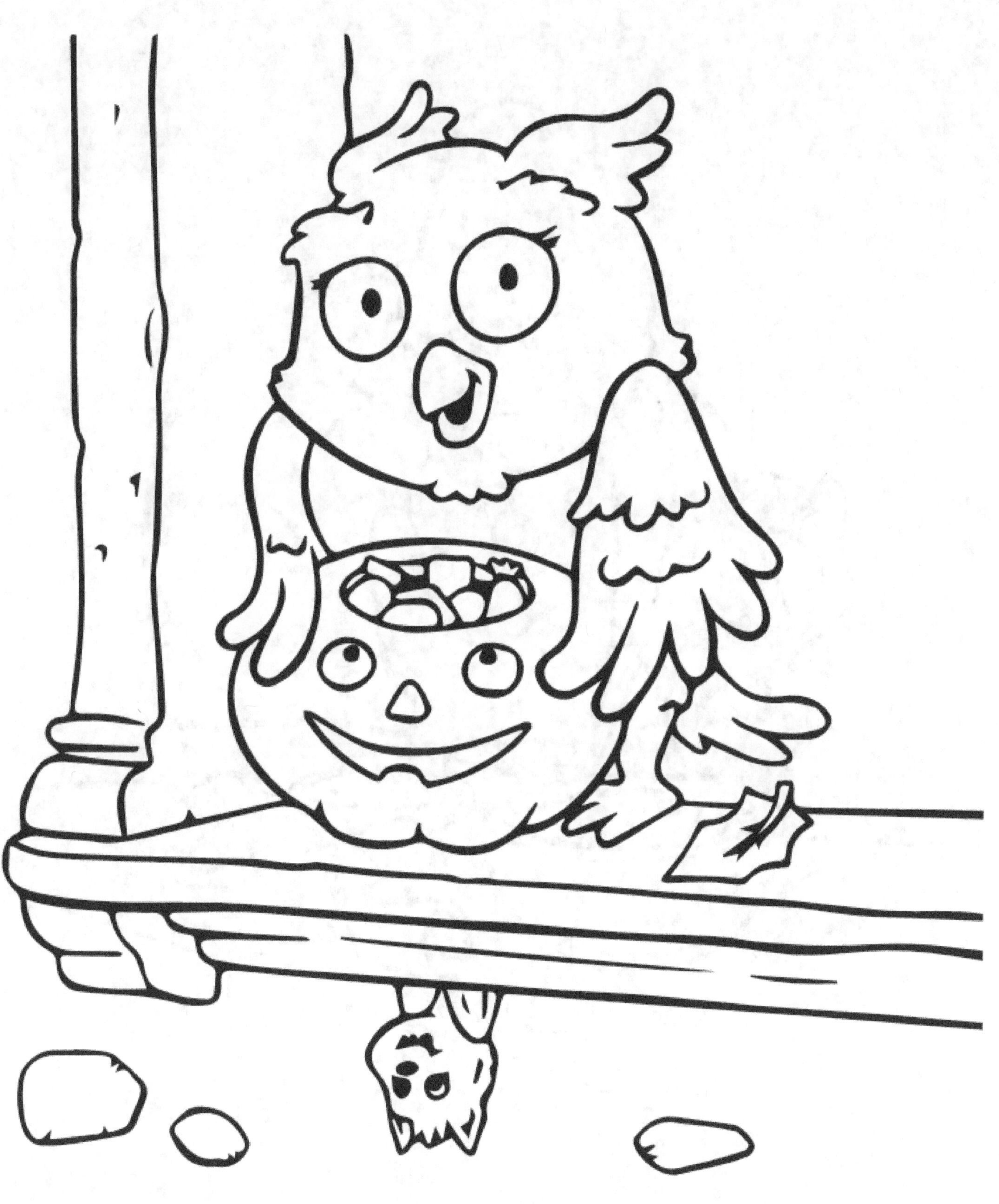

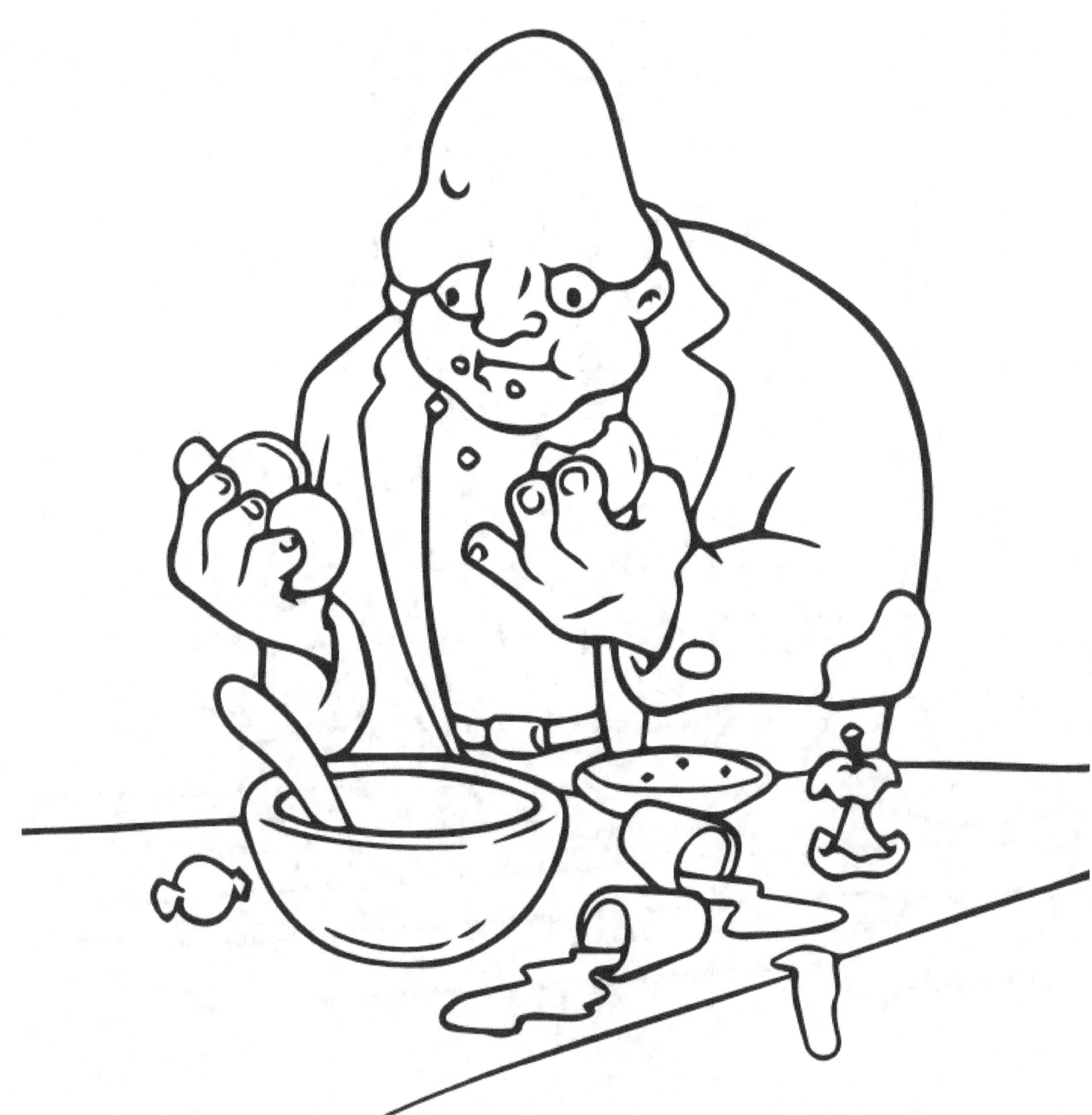

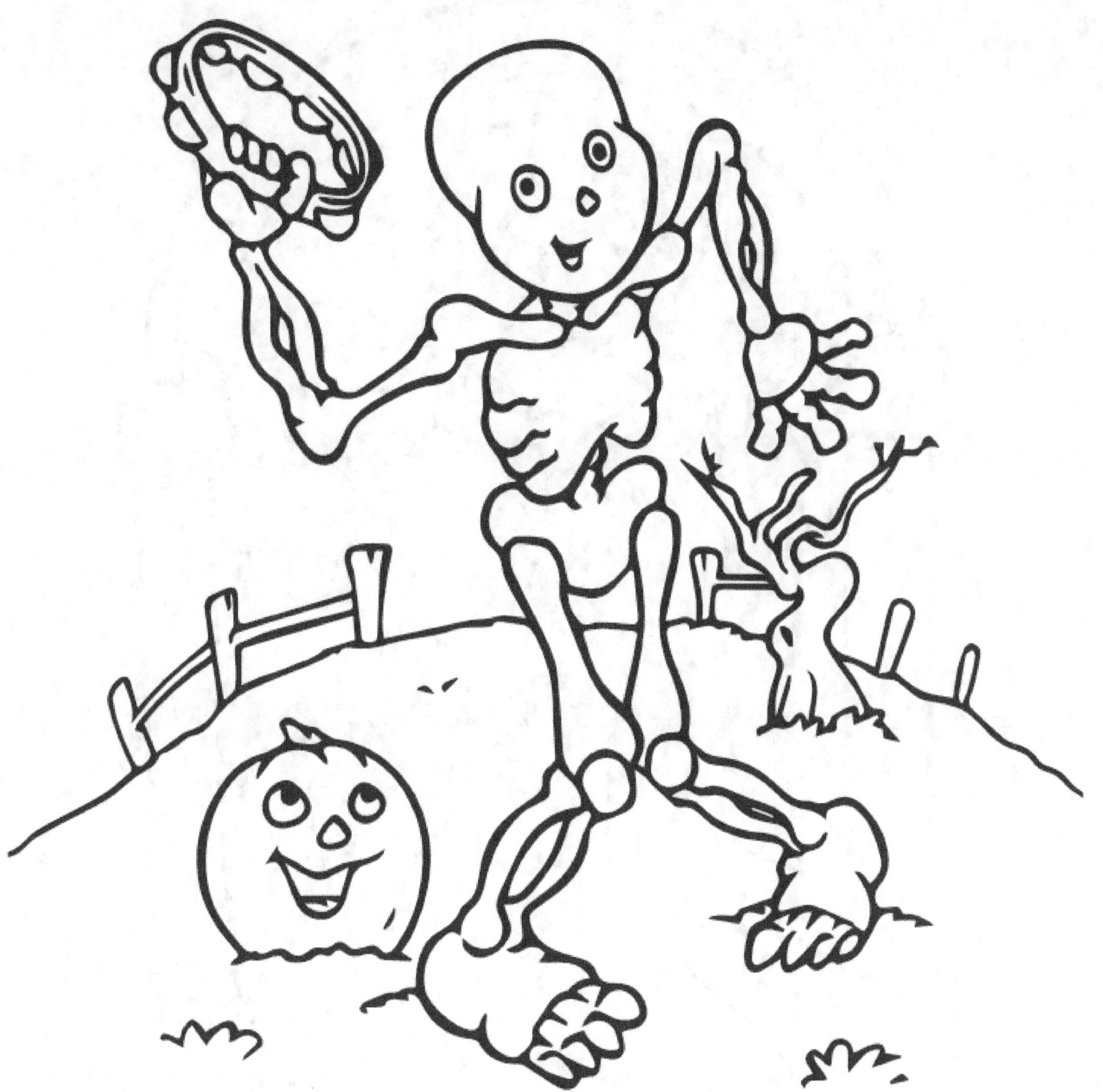

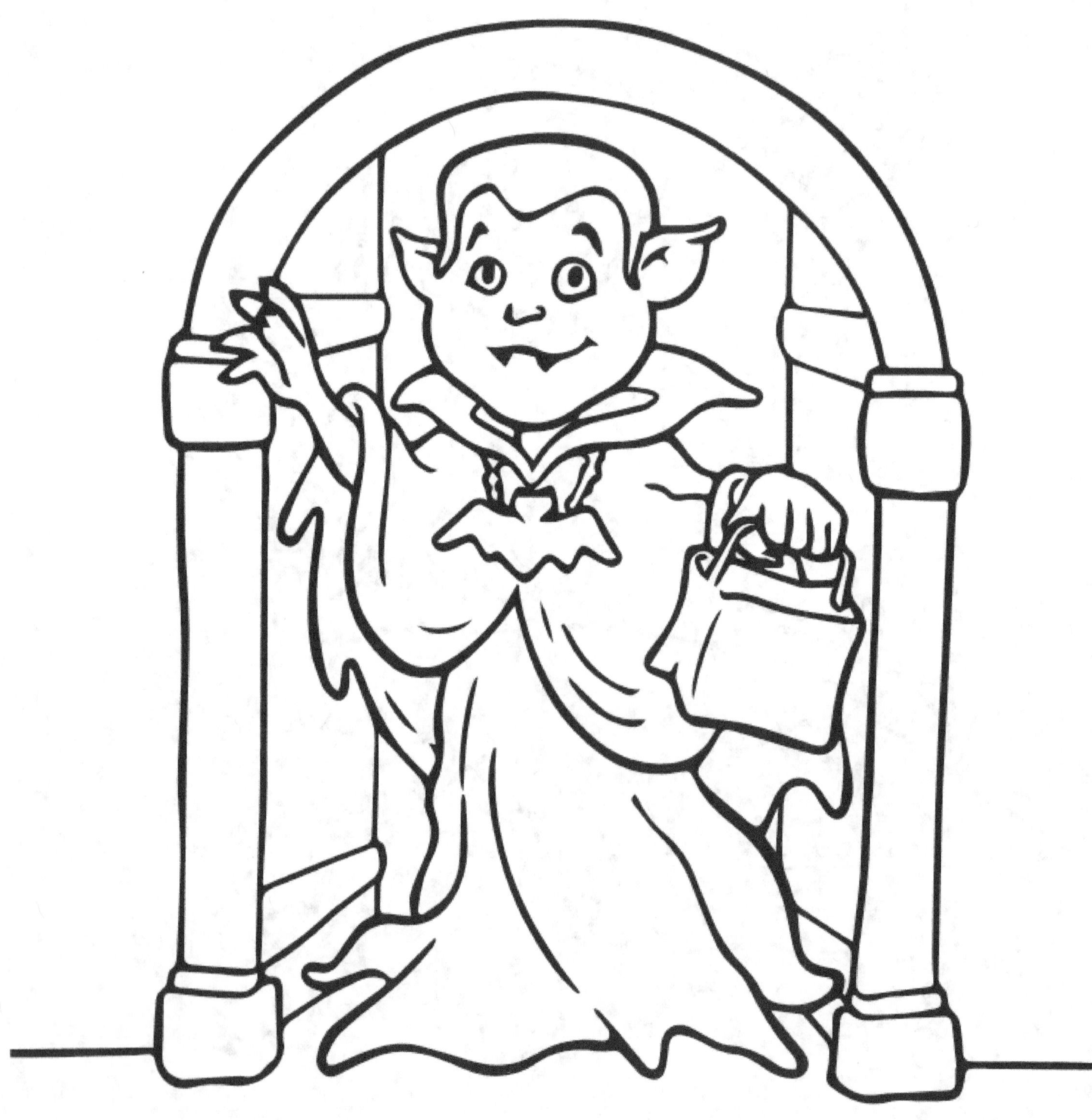

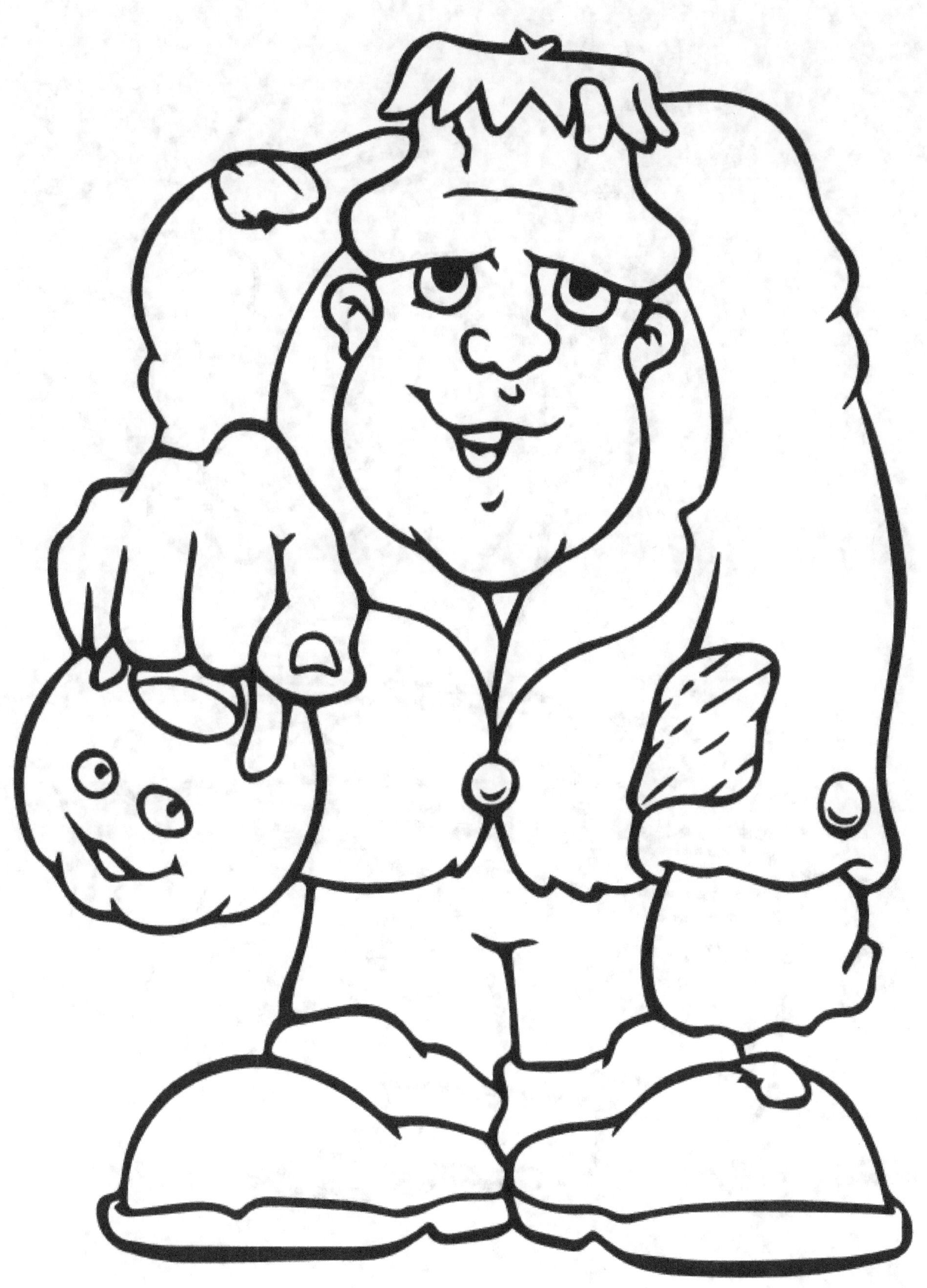

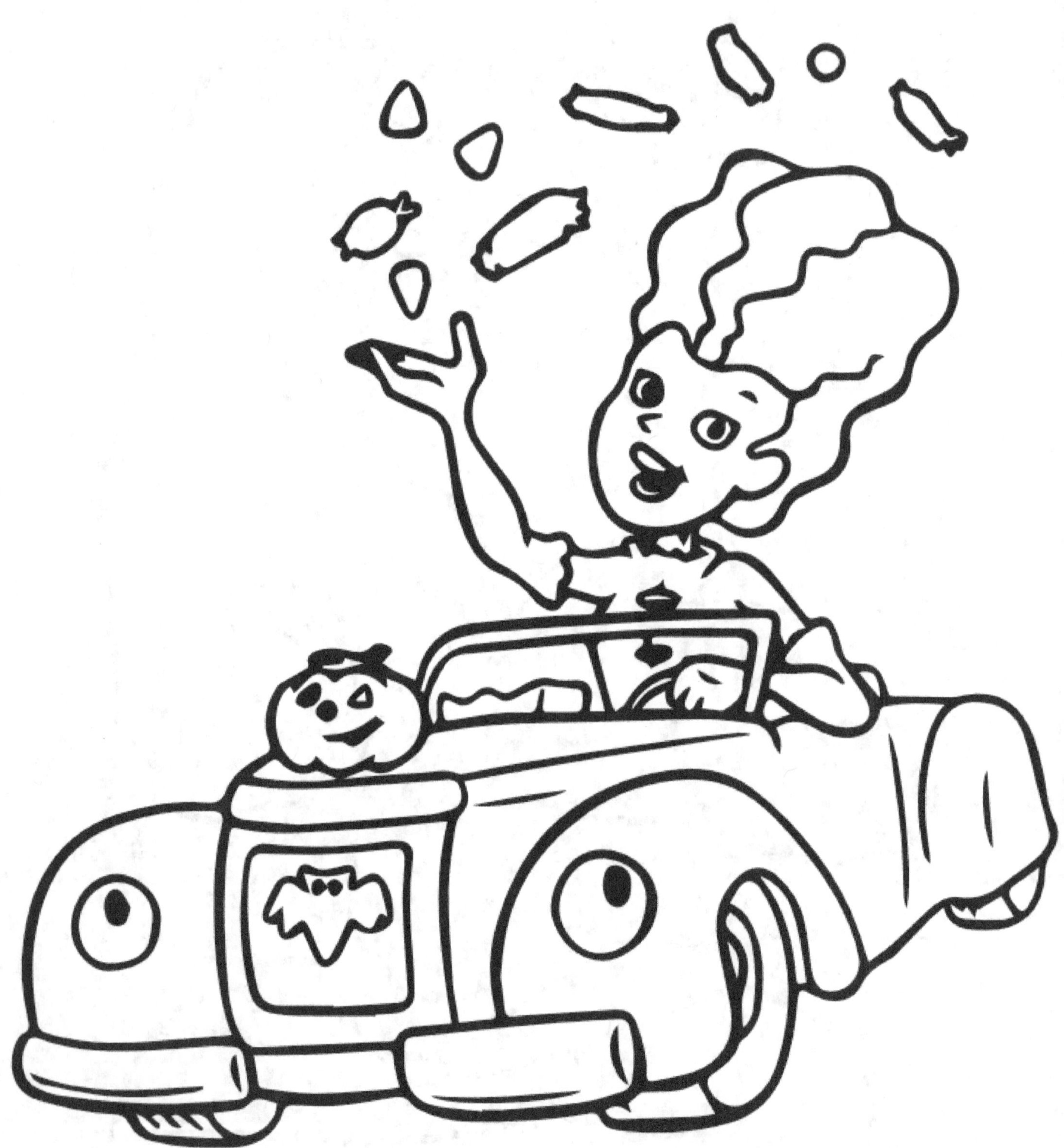

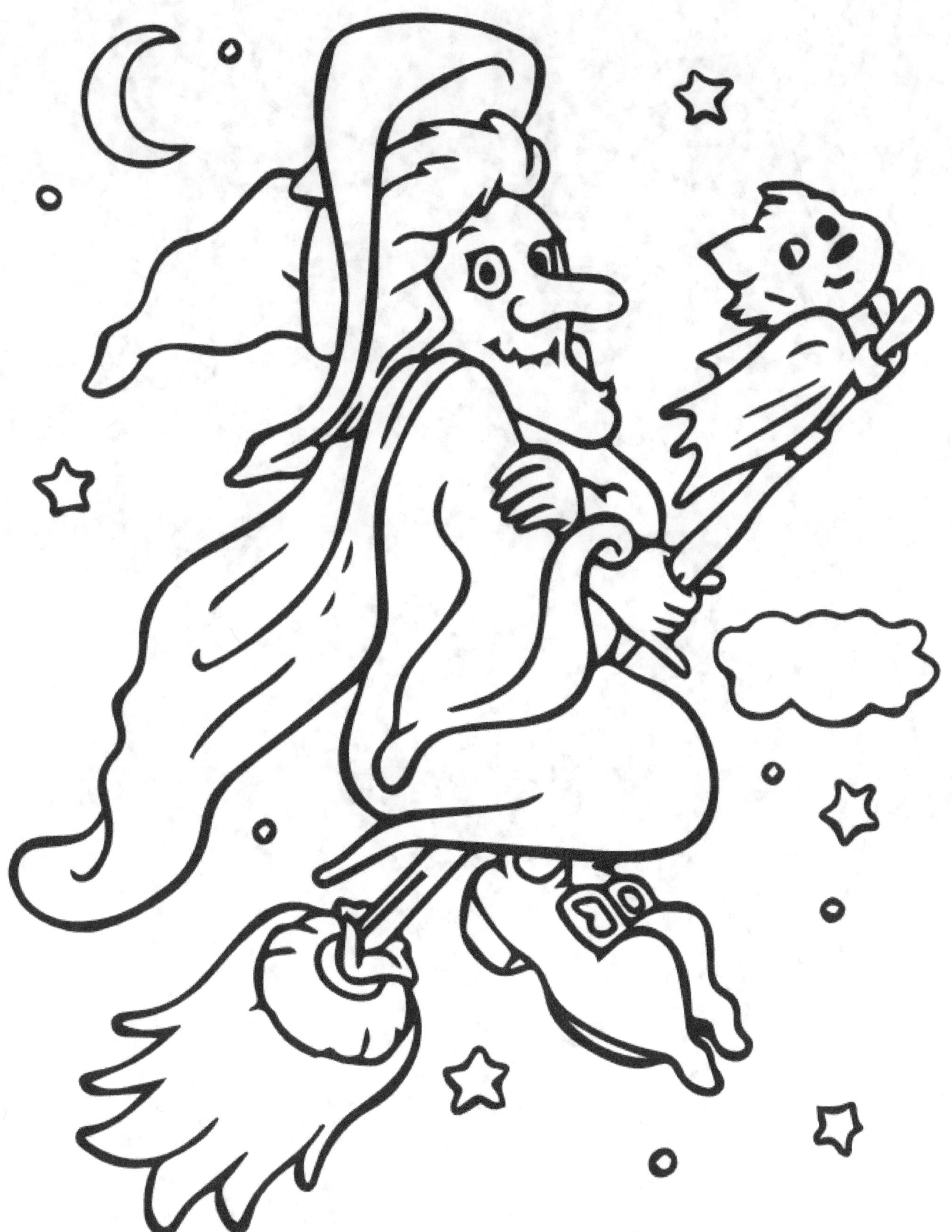

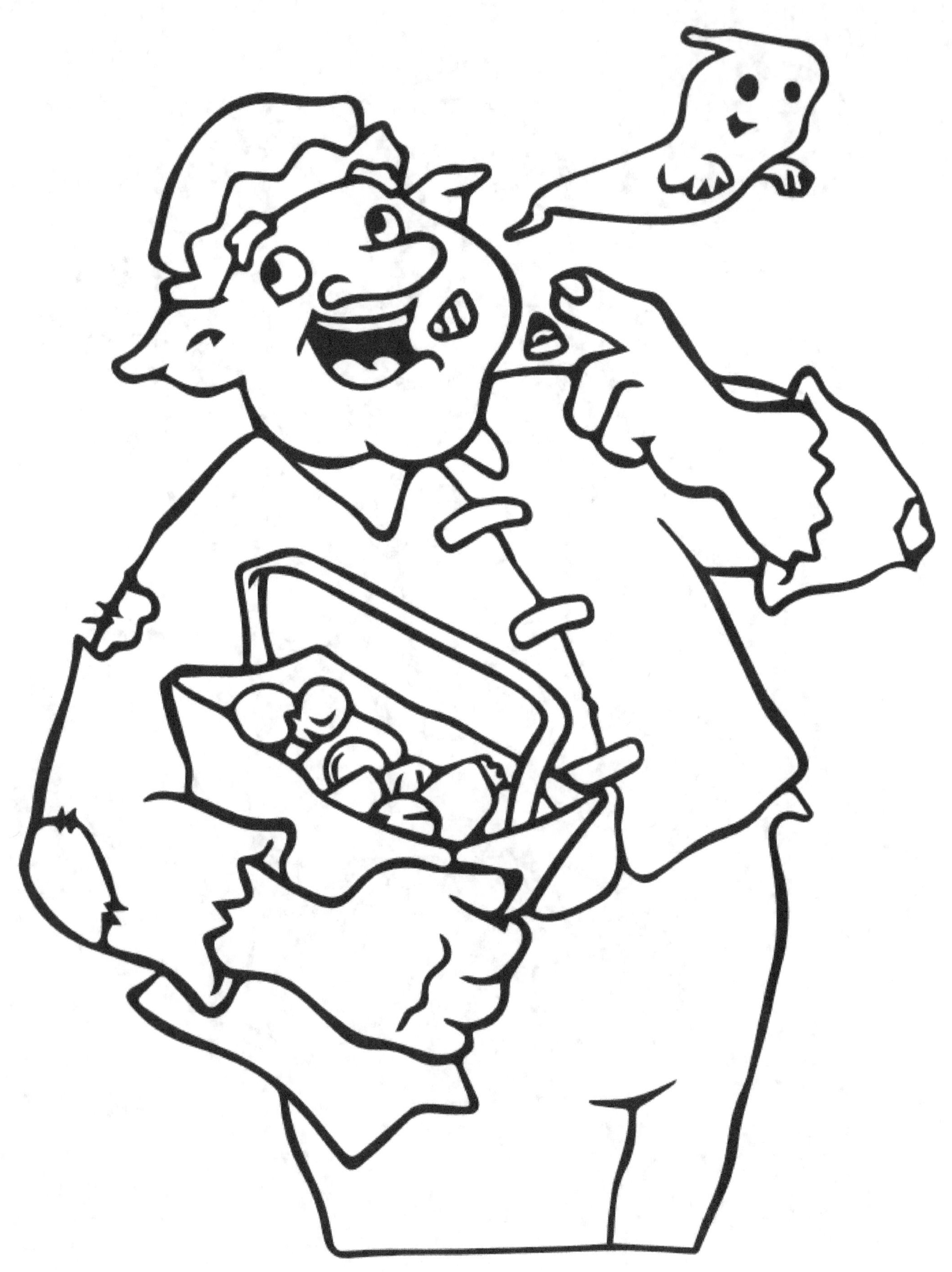

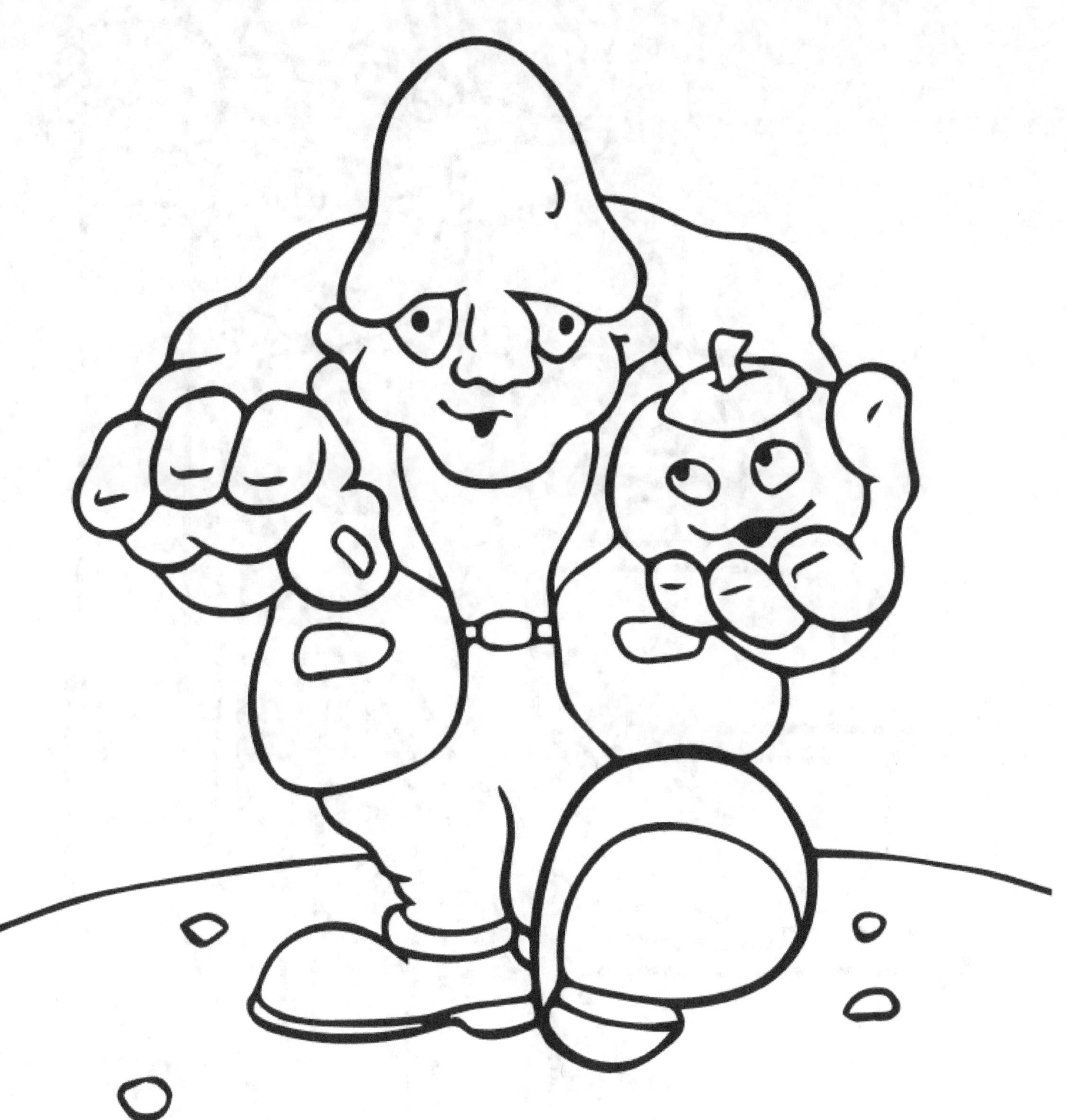

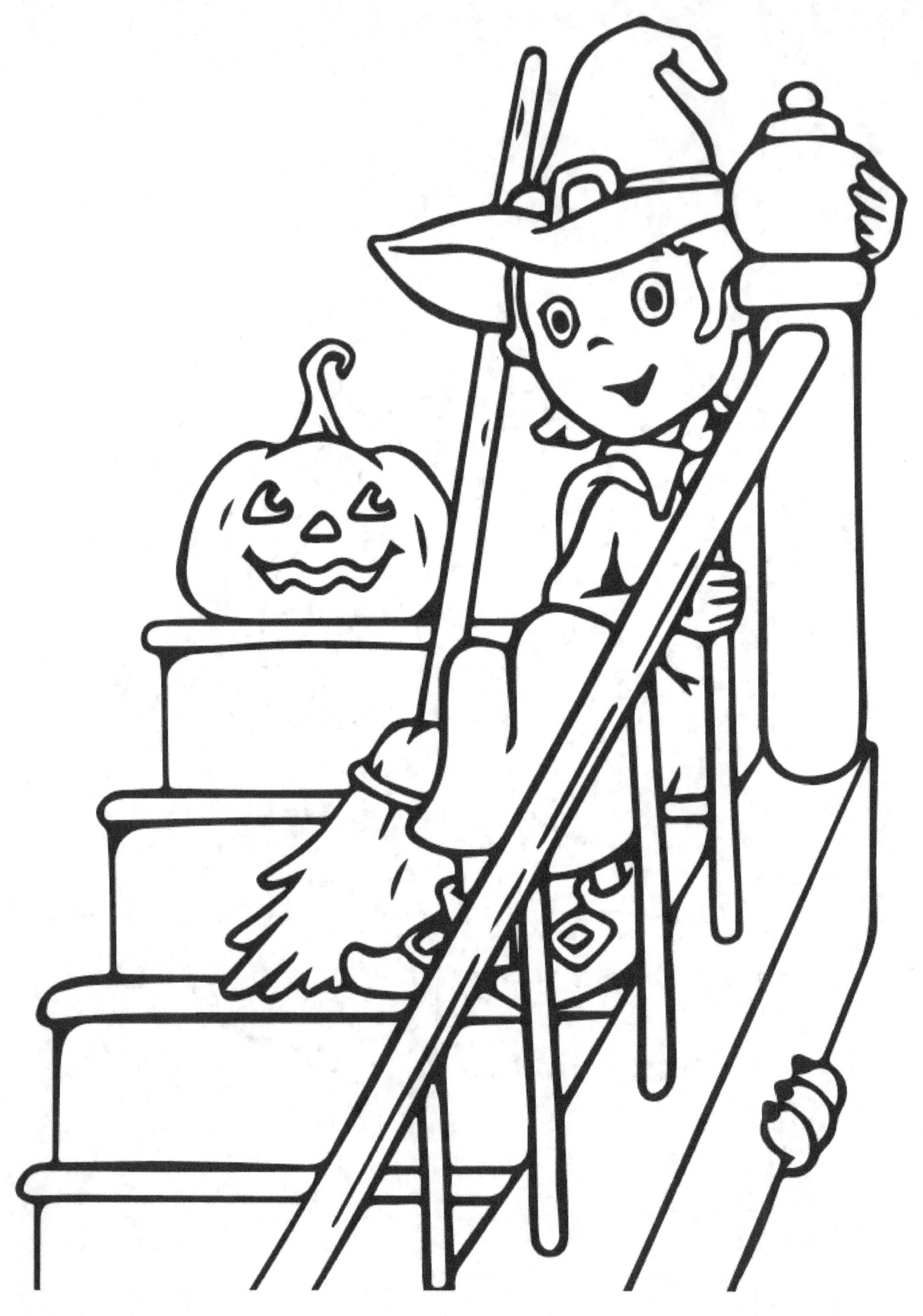

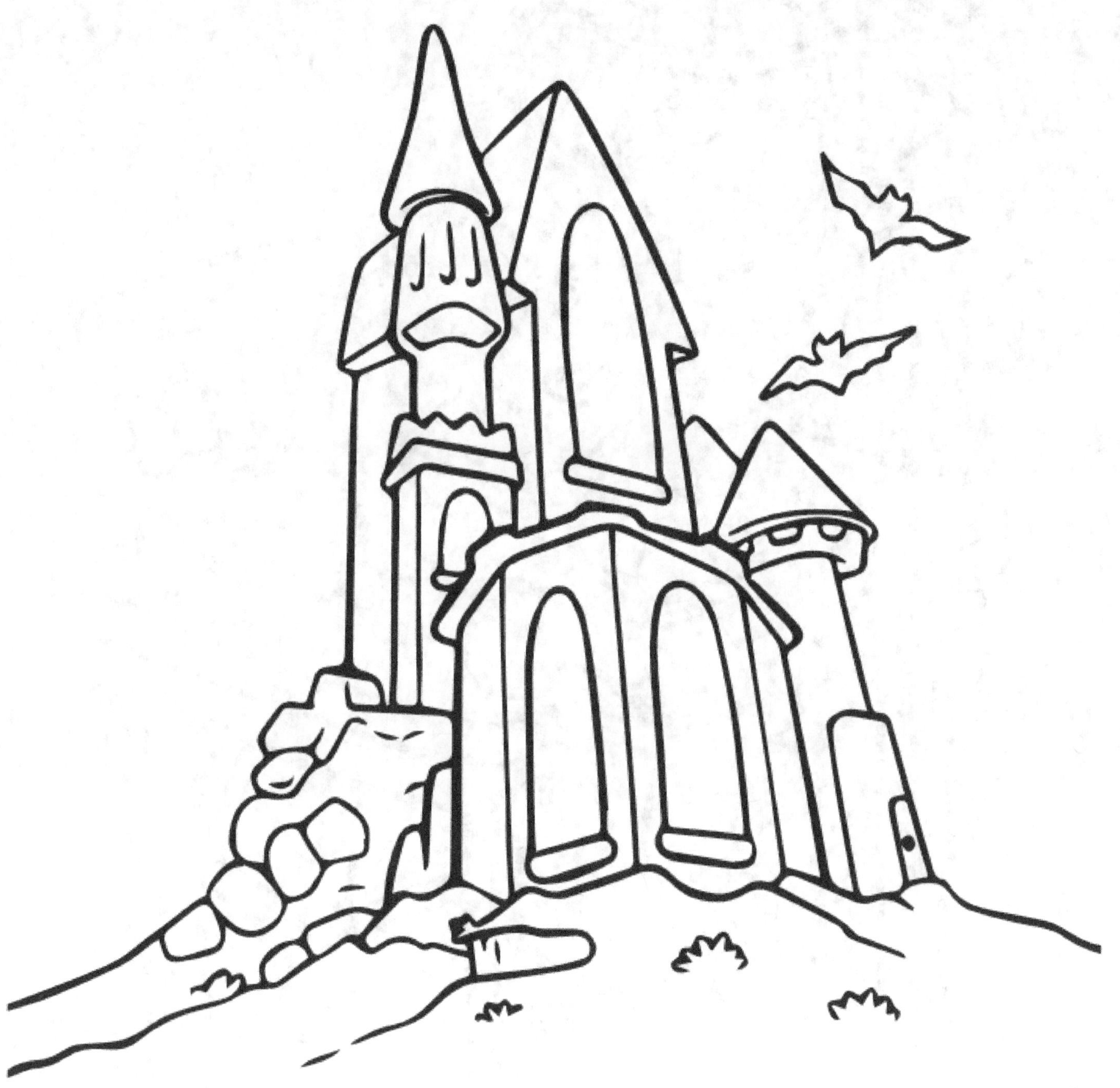

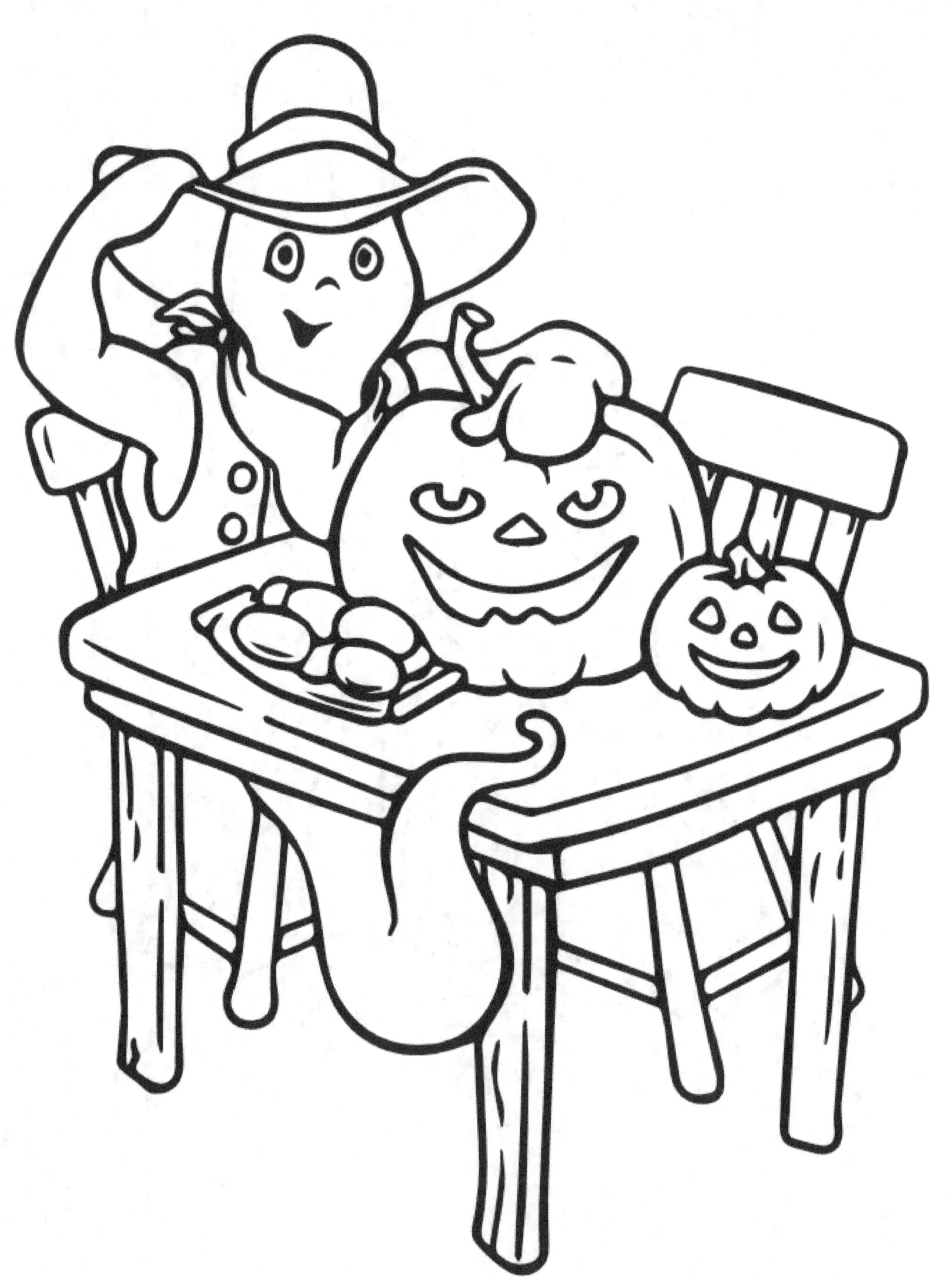

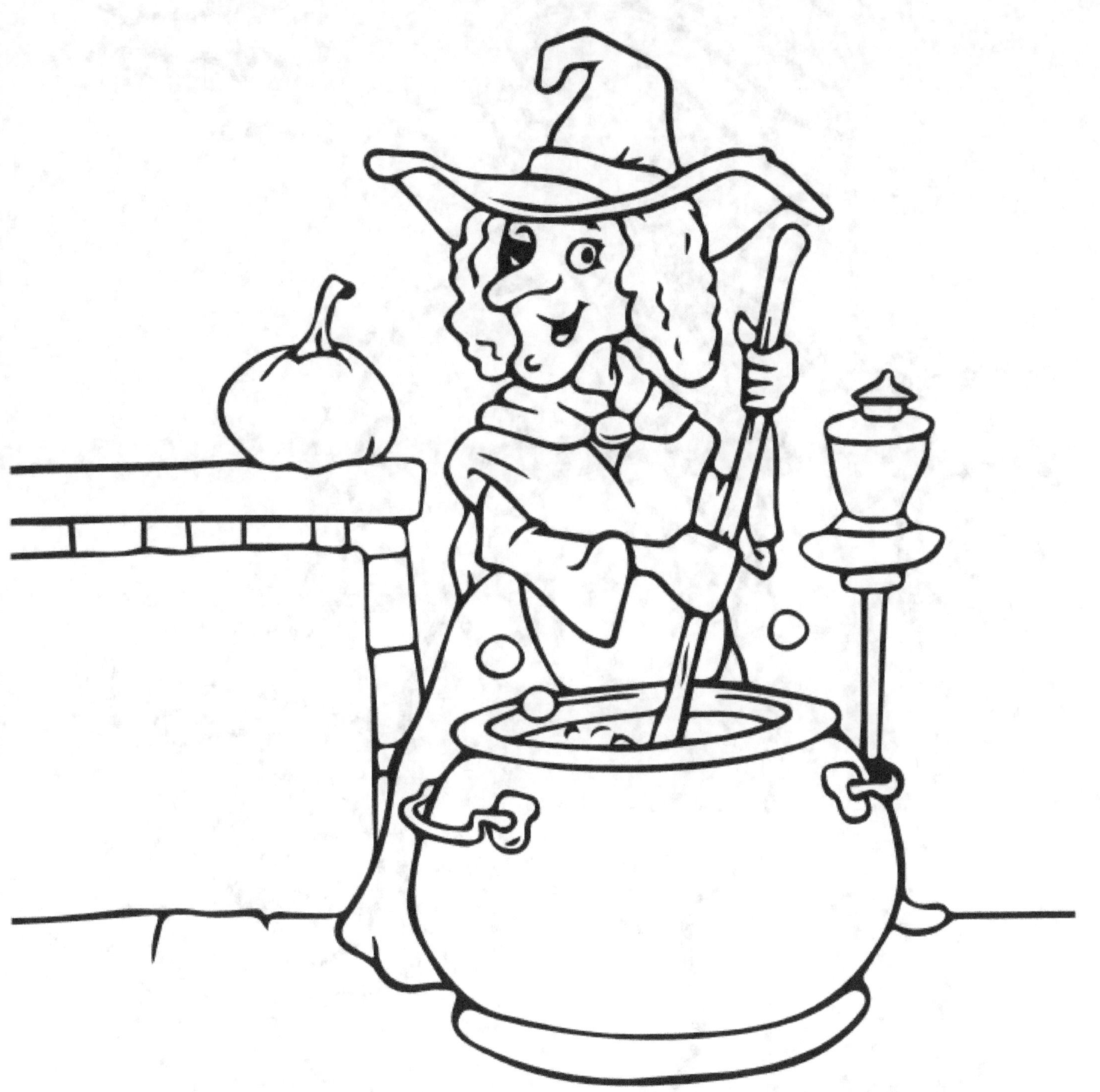

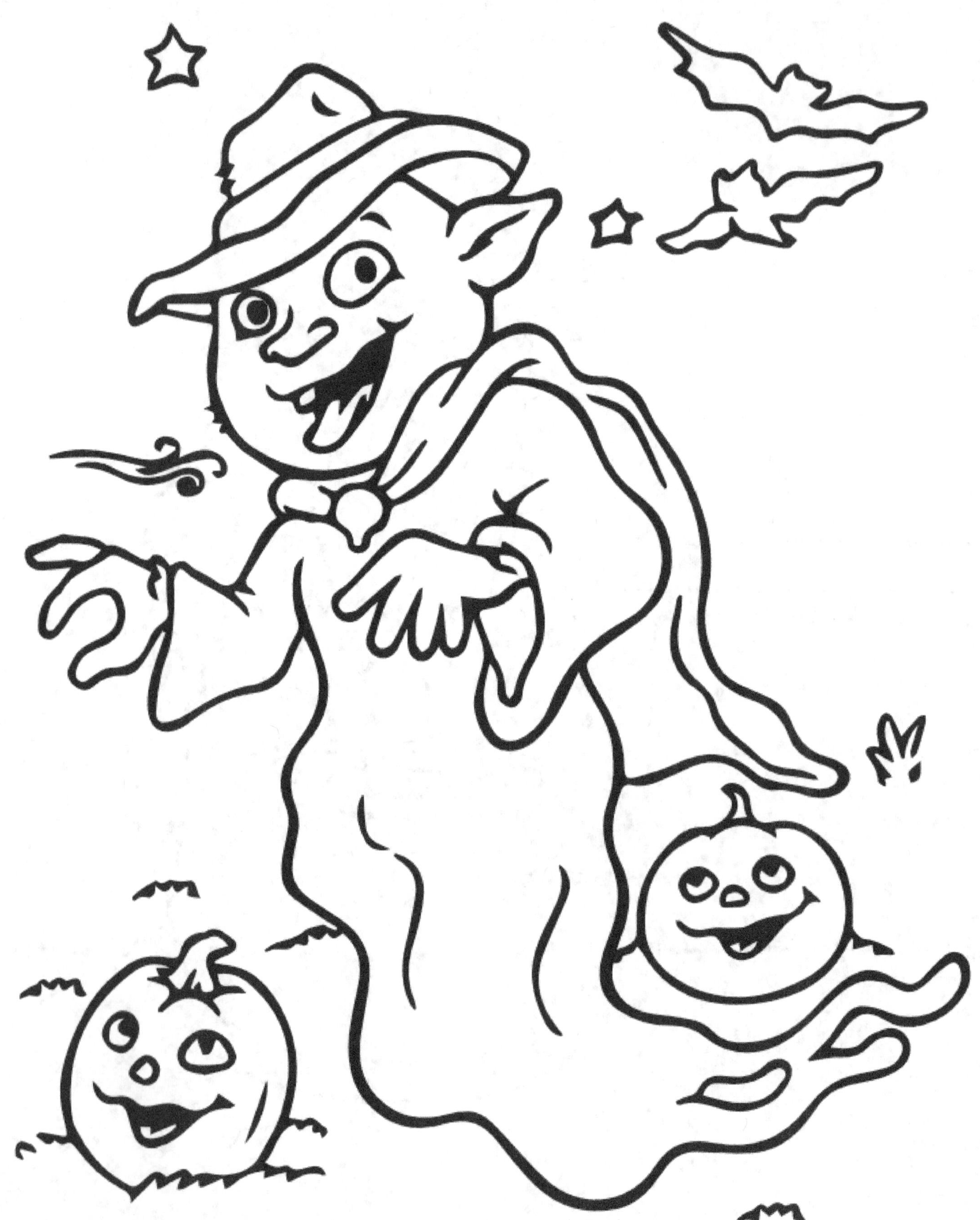

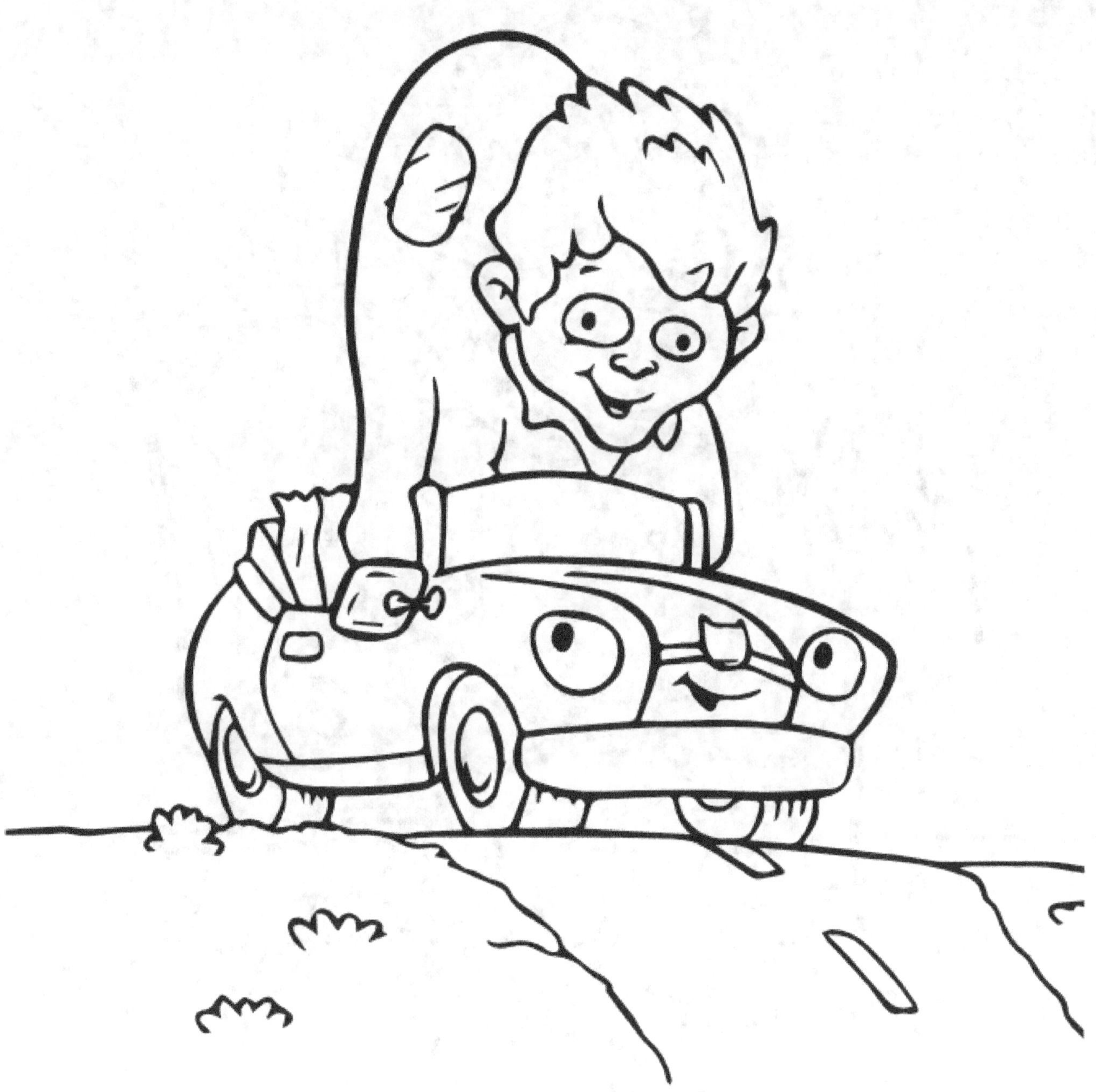

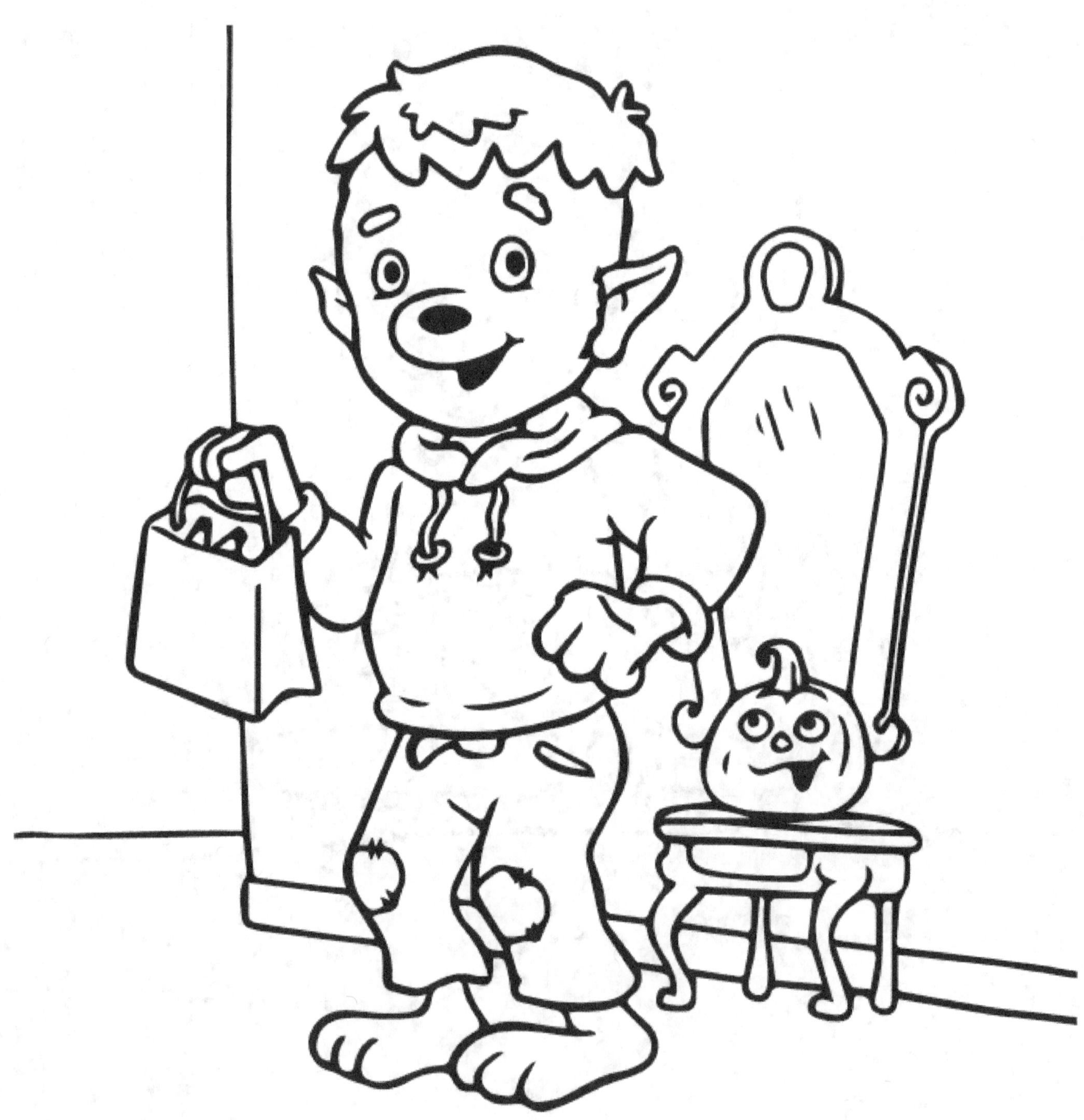

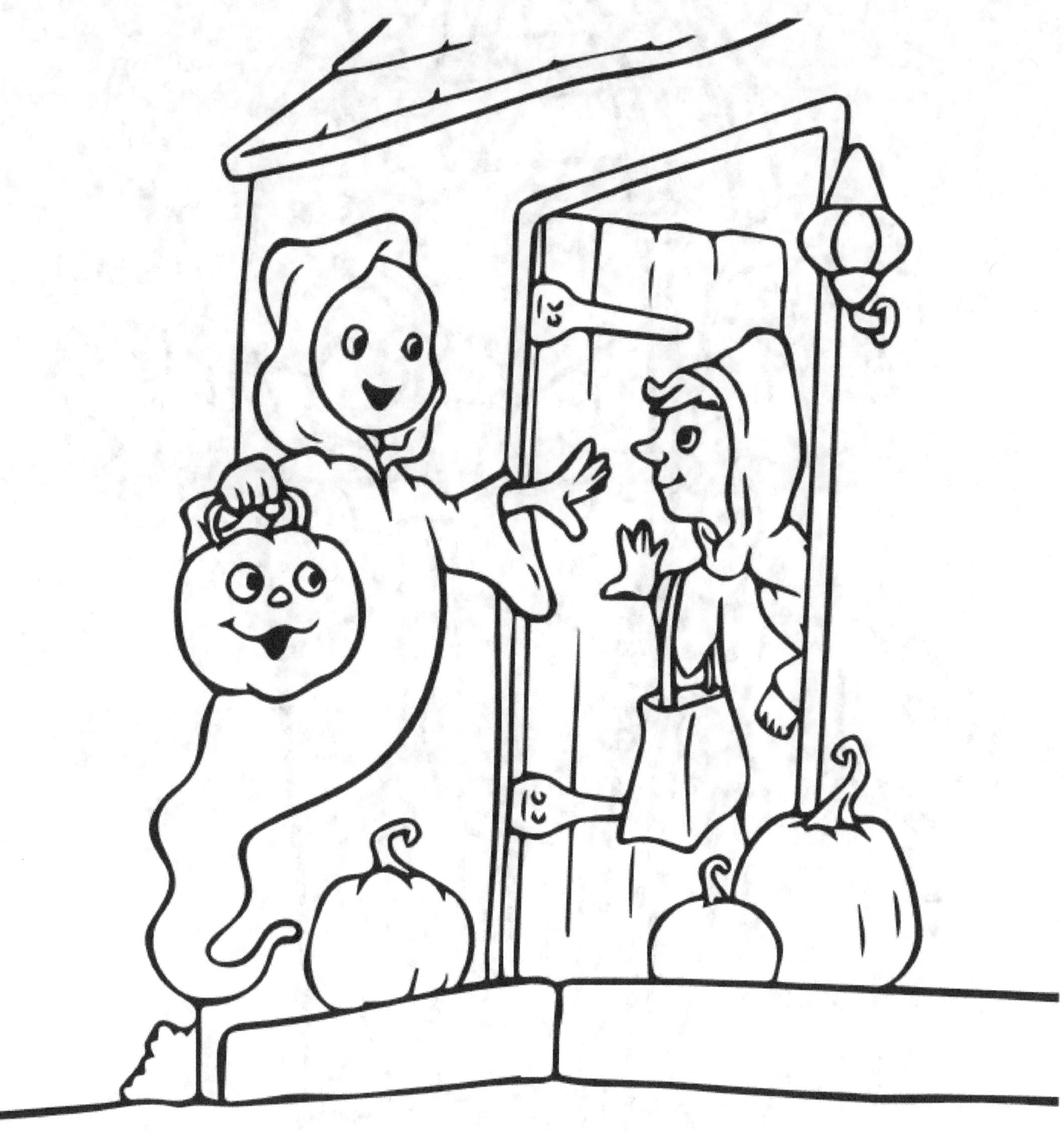

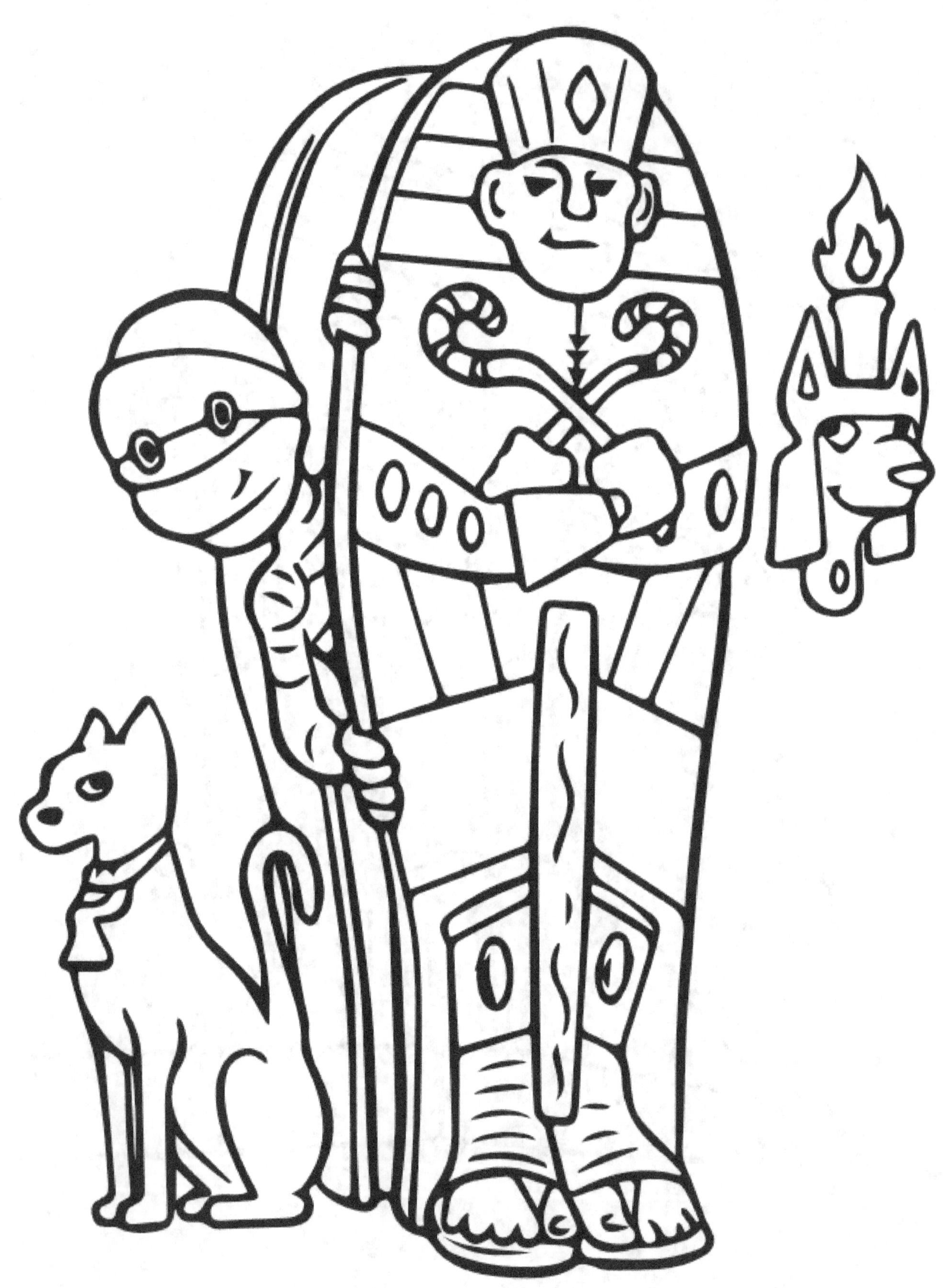

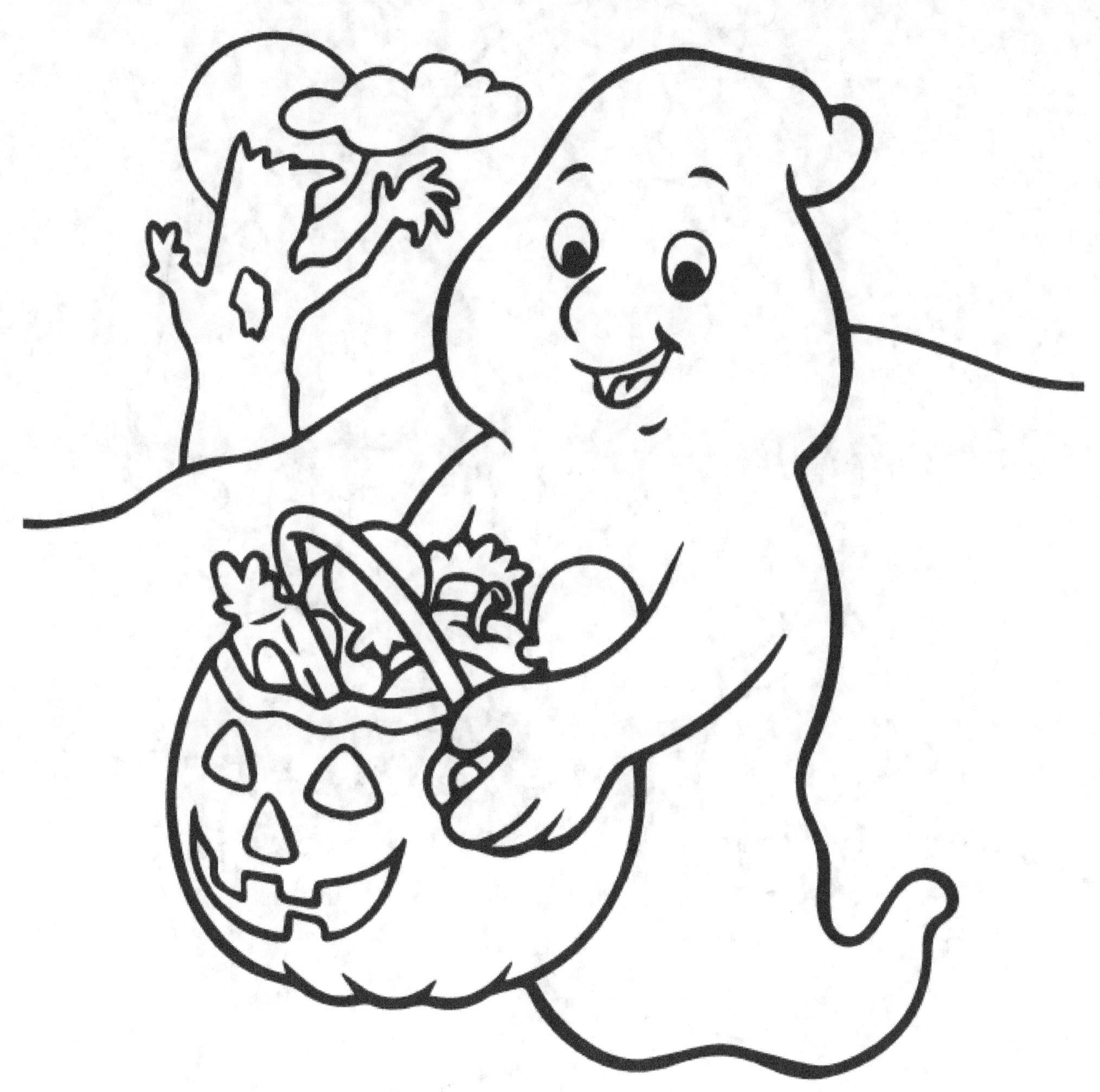

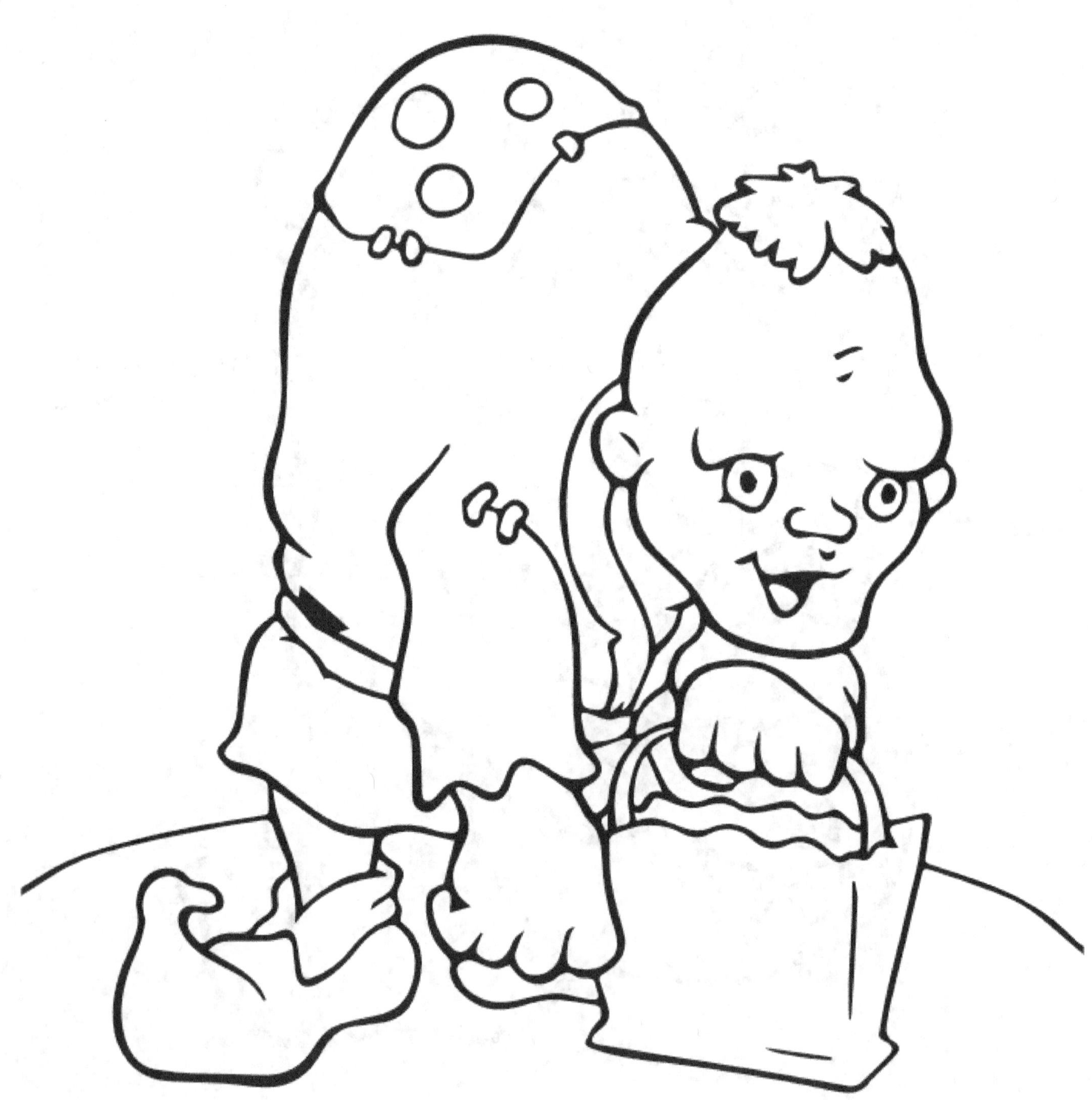

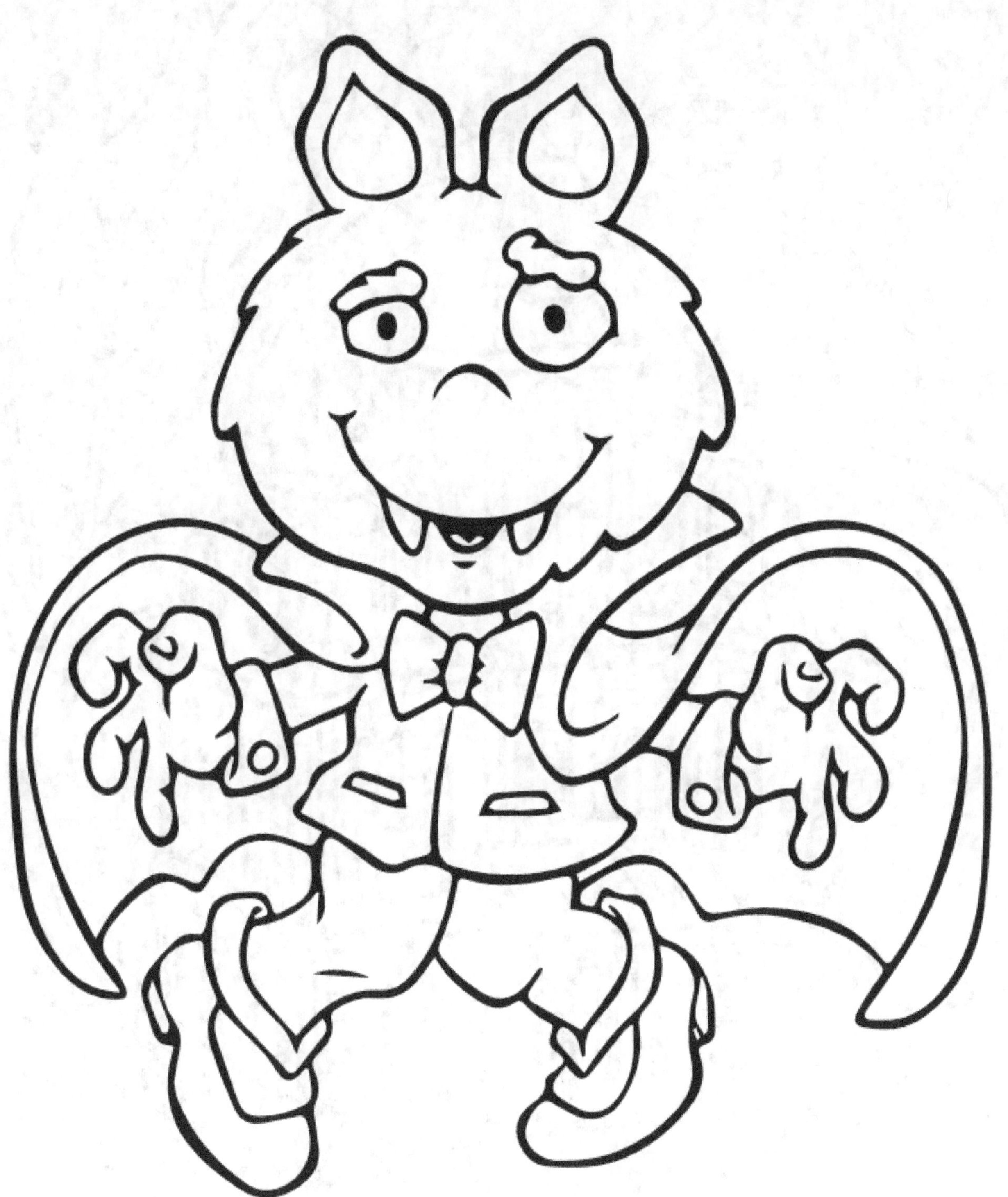

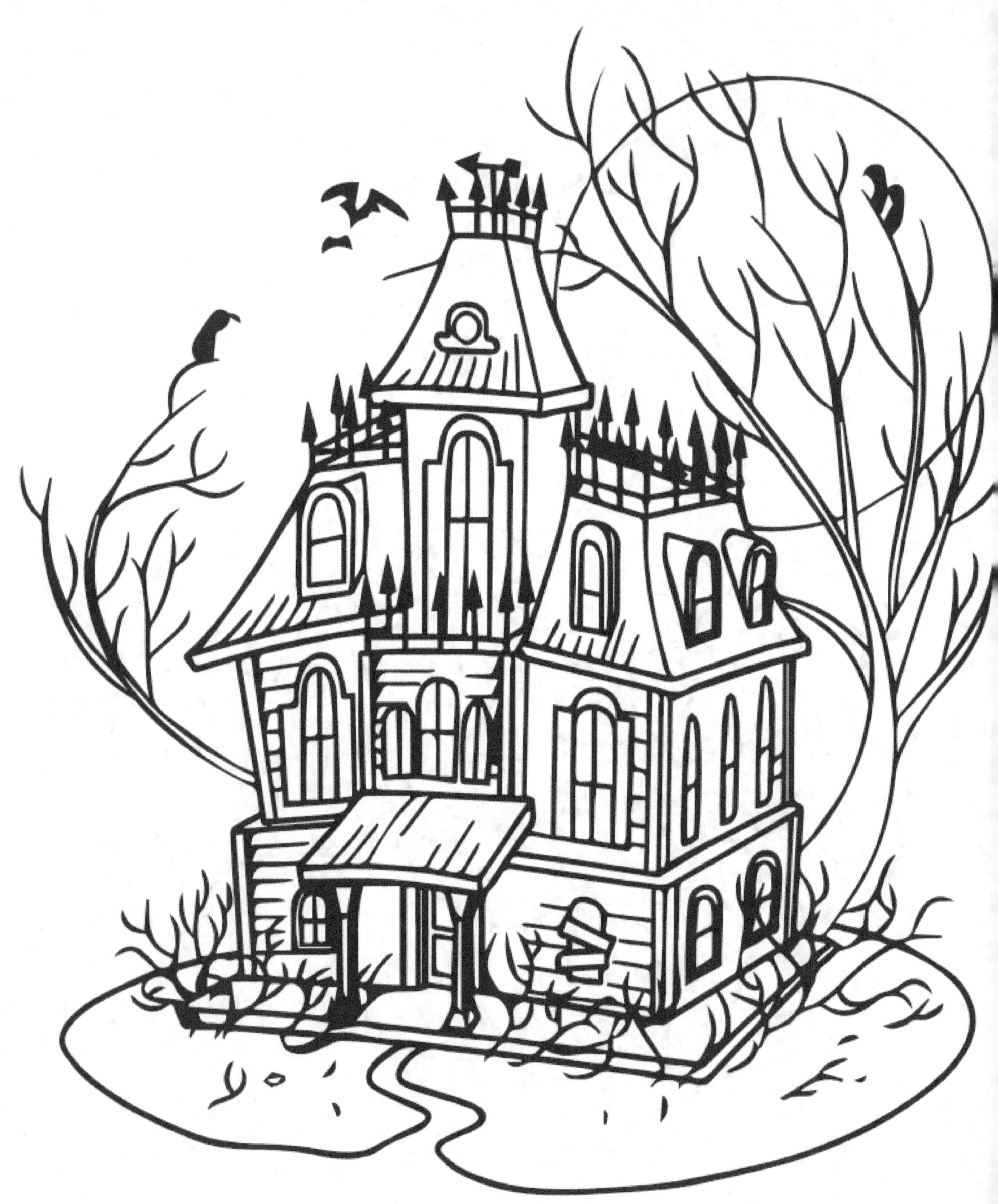

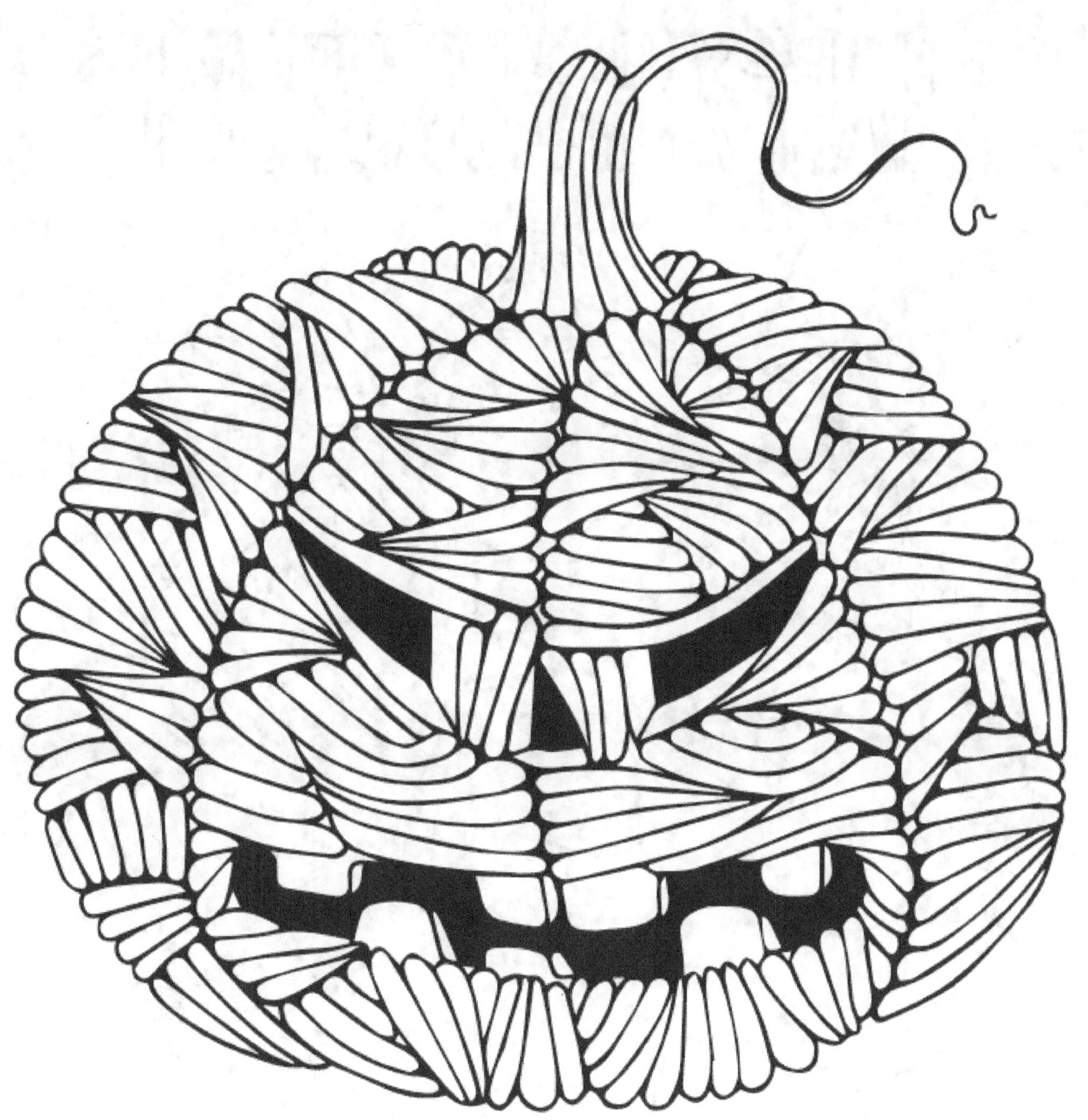

HAPPY HALLOWEEN !

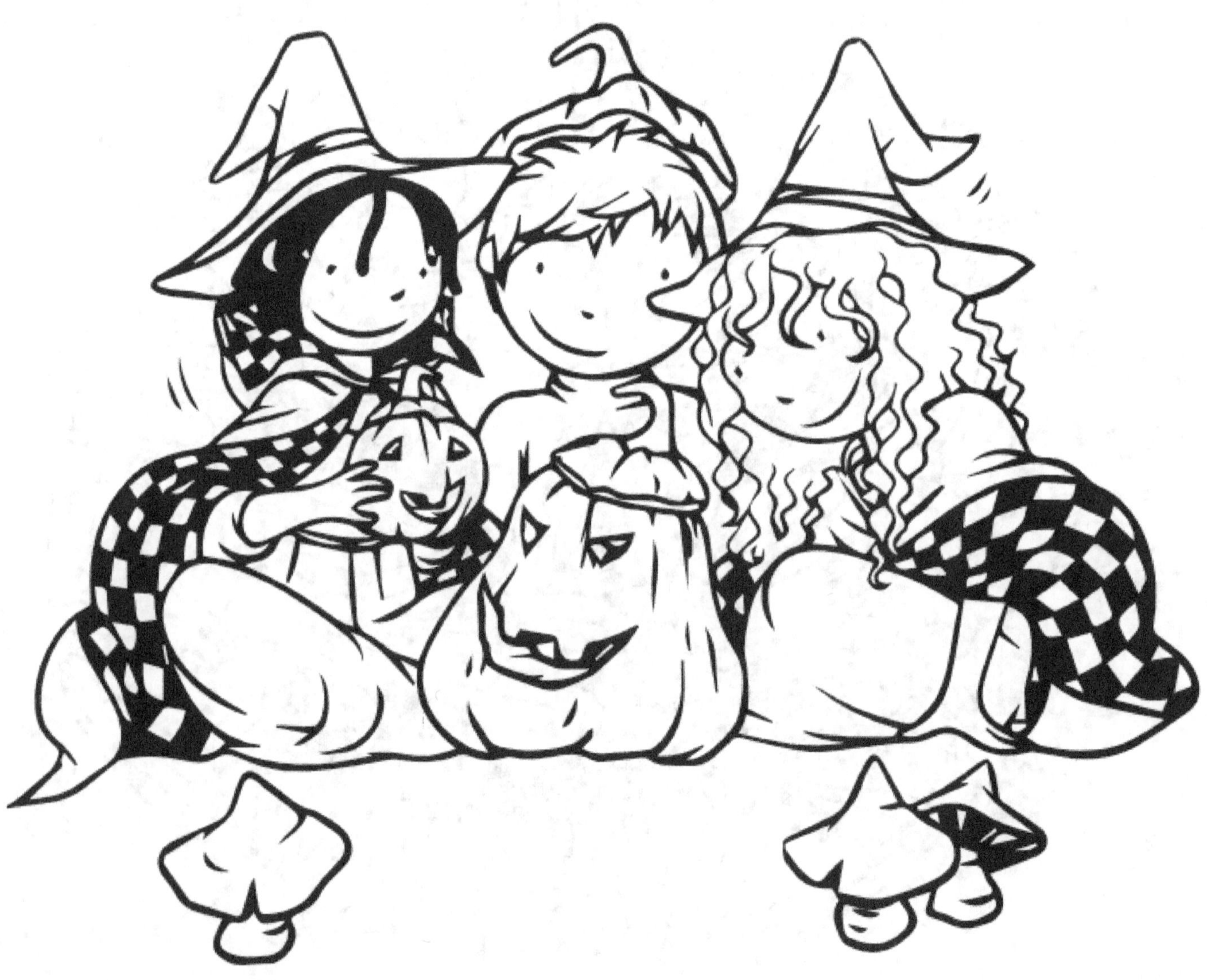

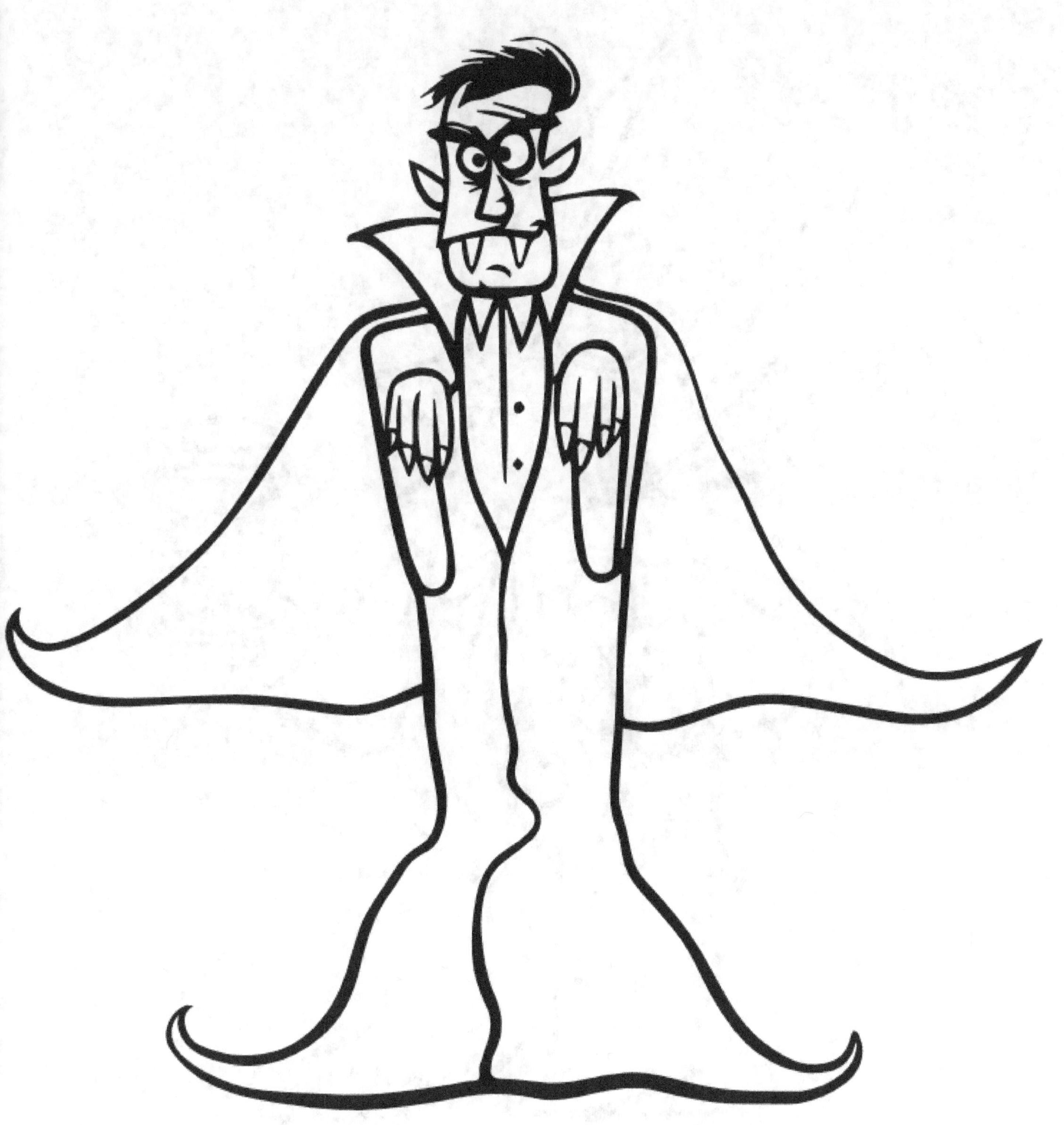

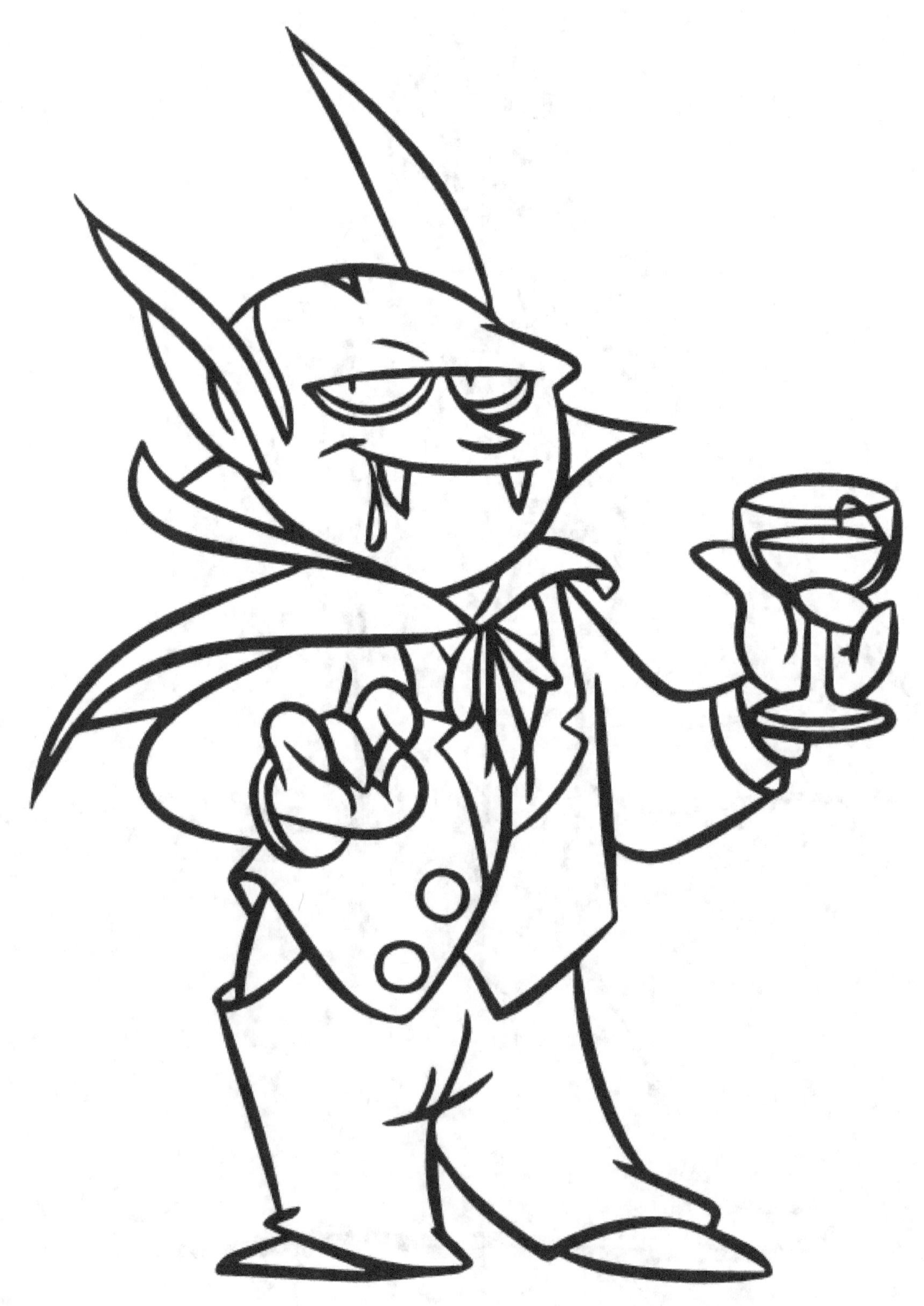

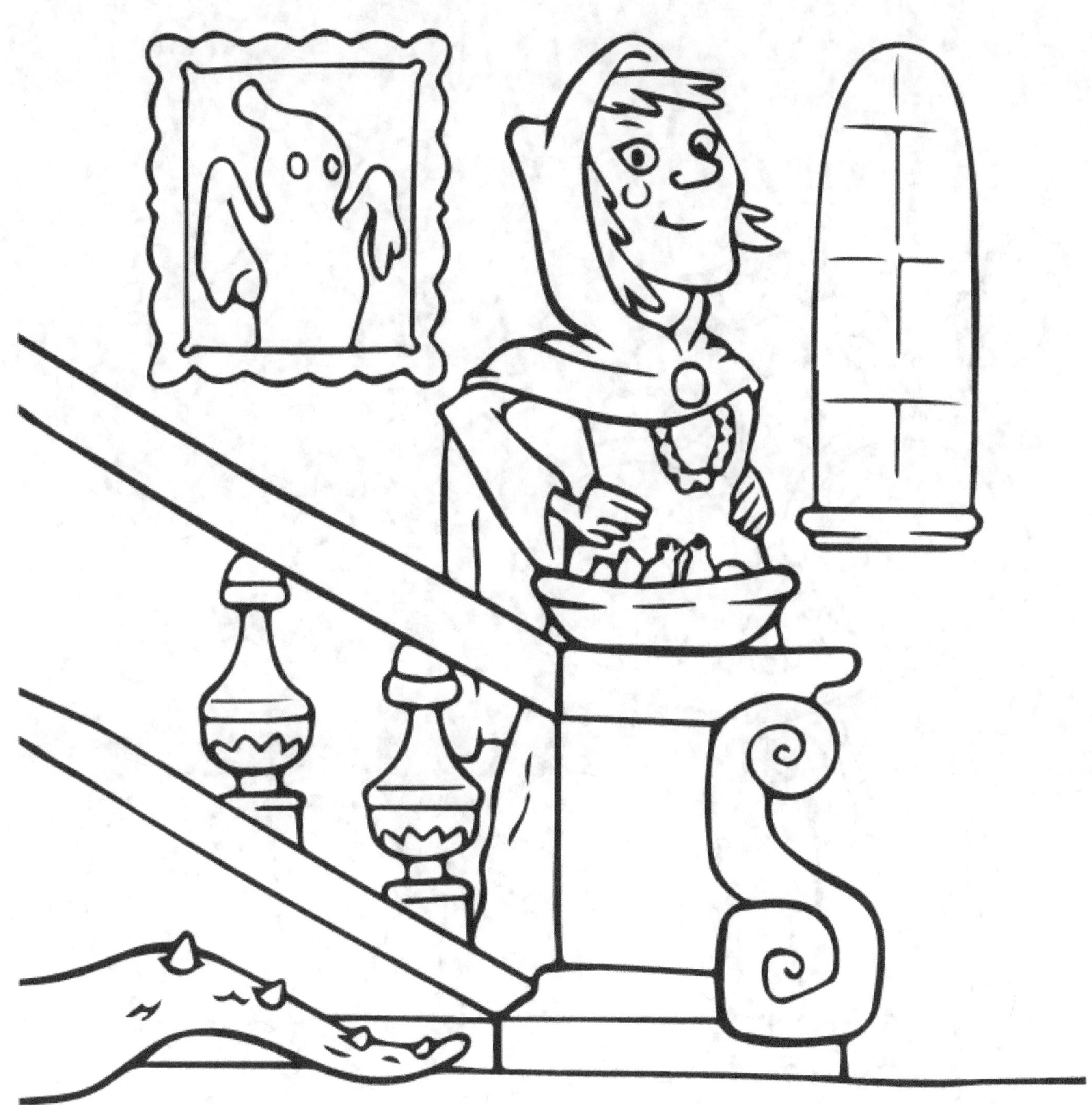

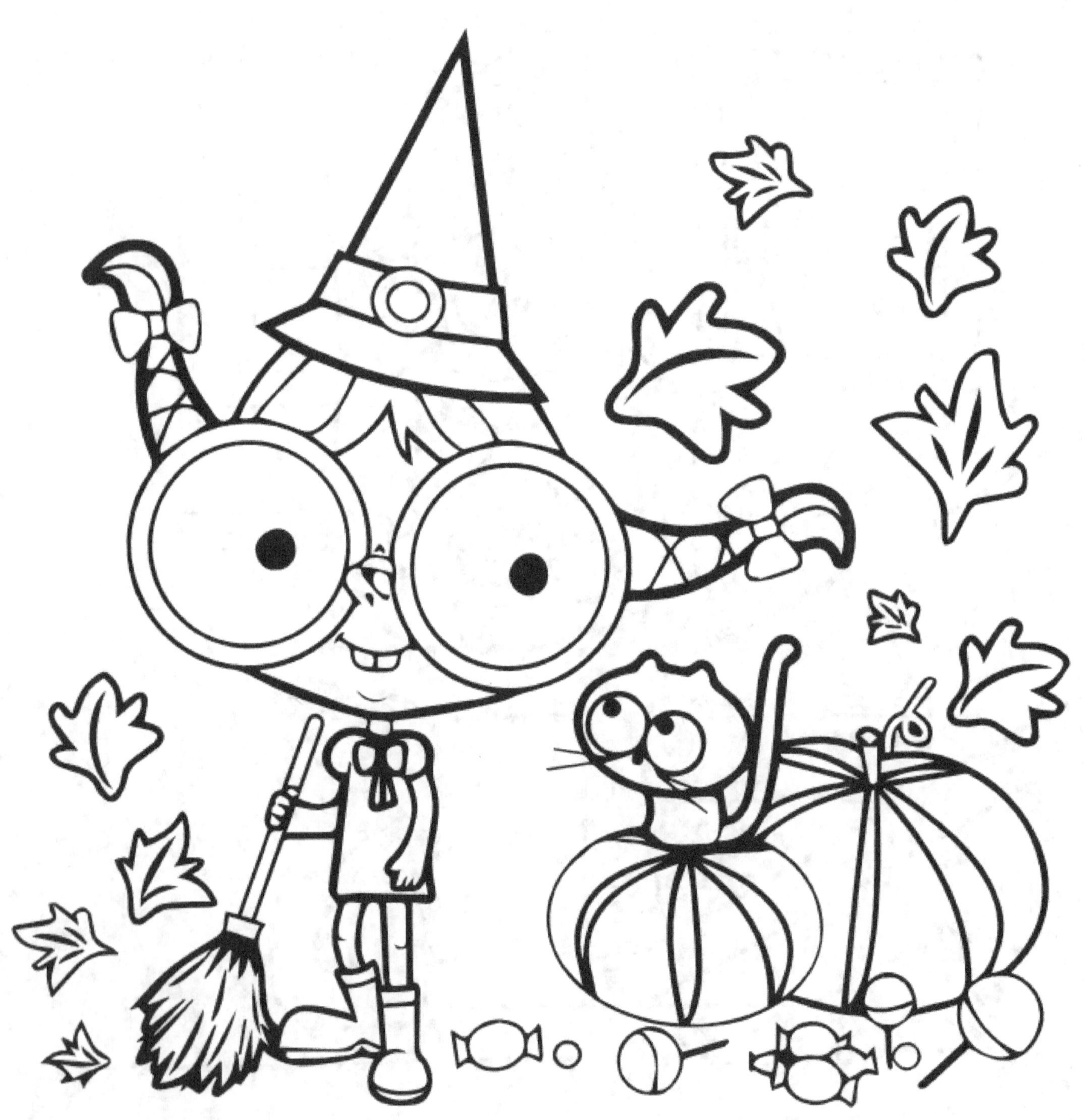

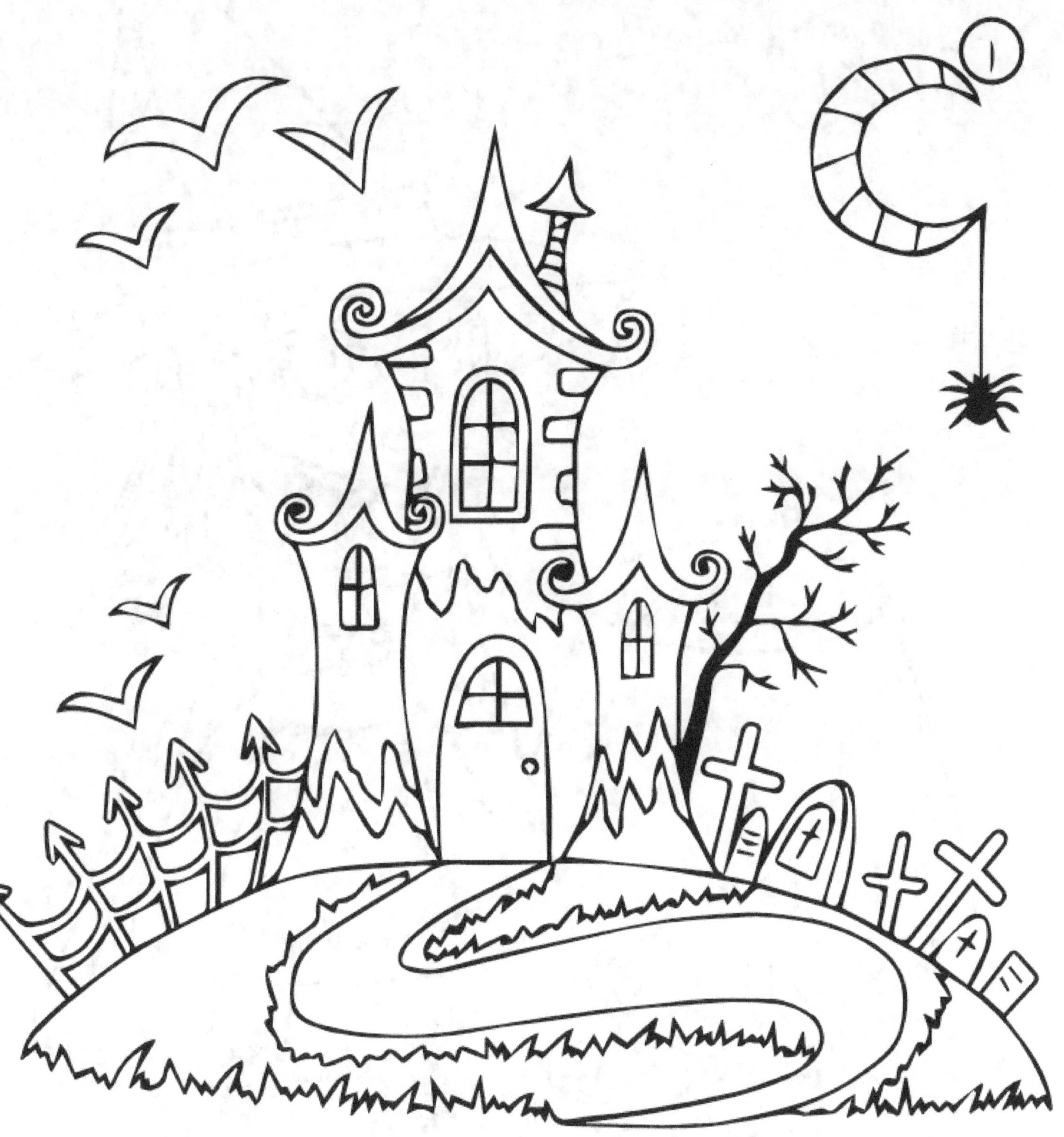

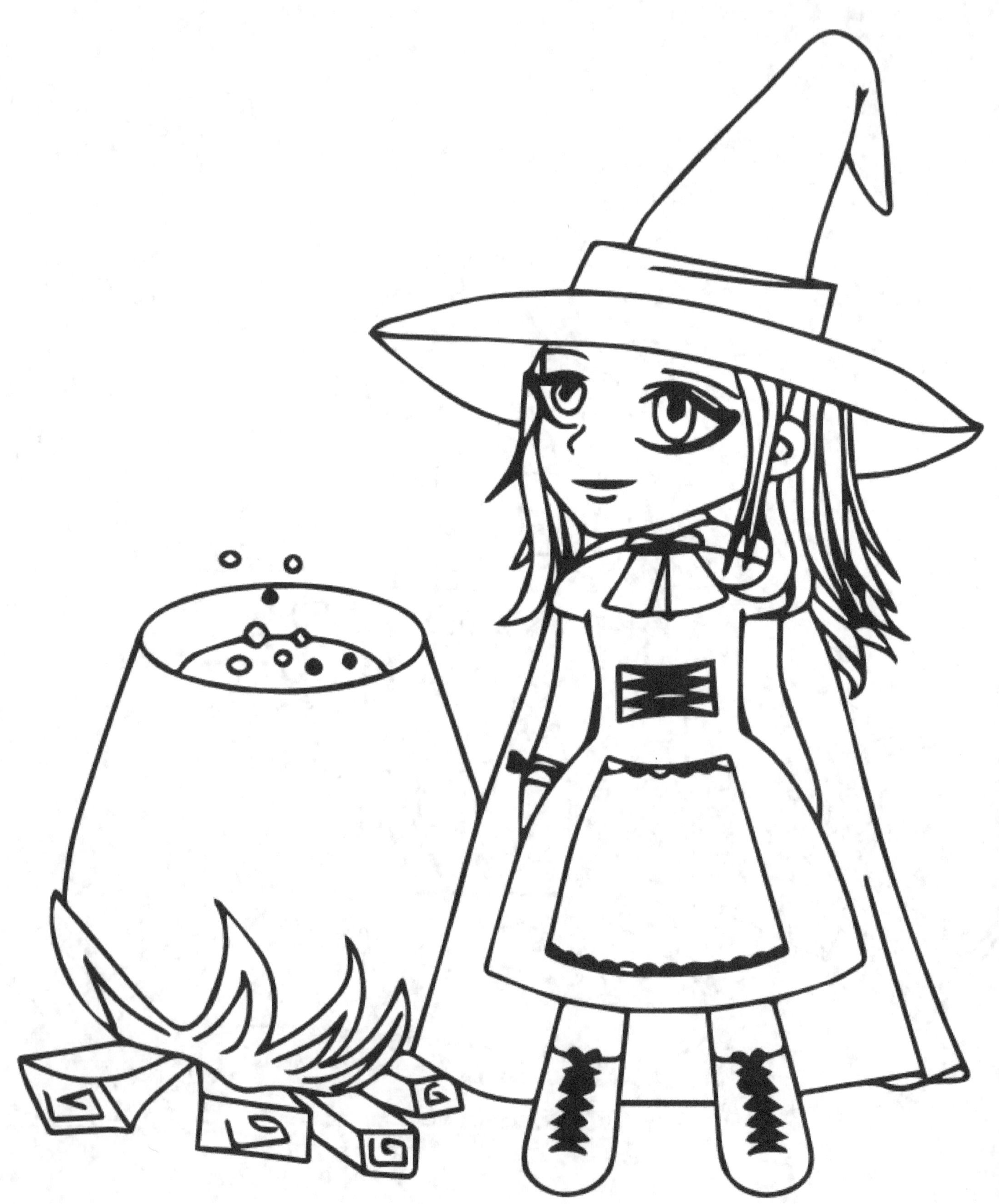

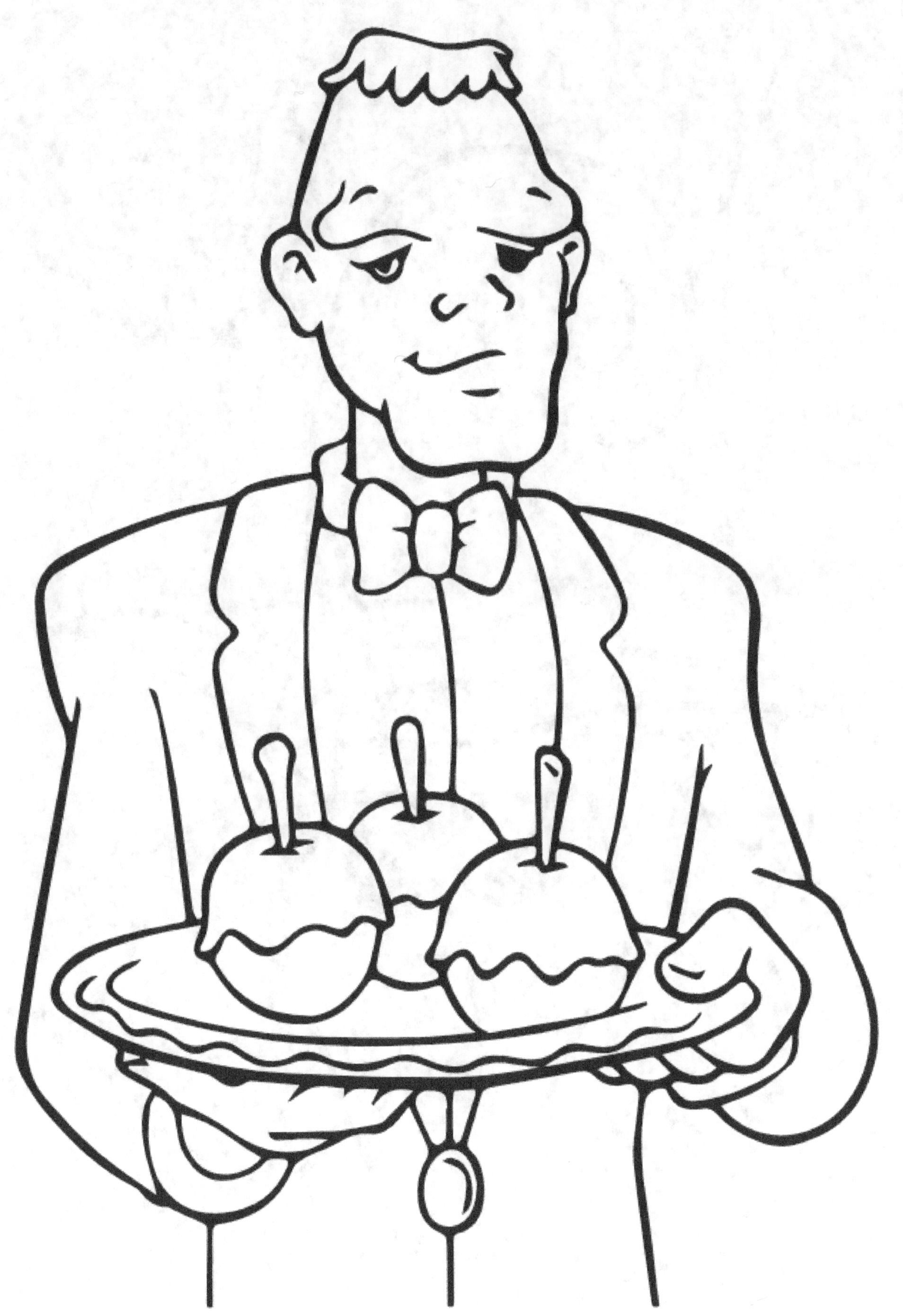

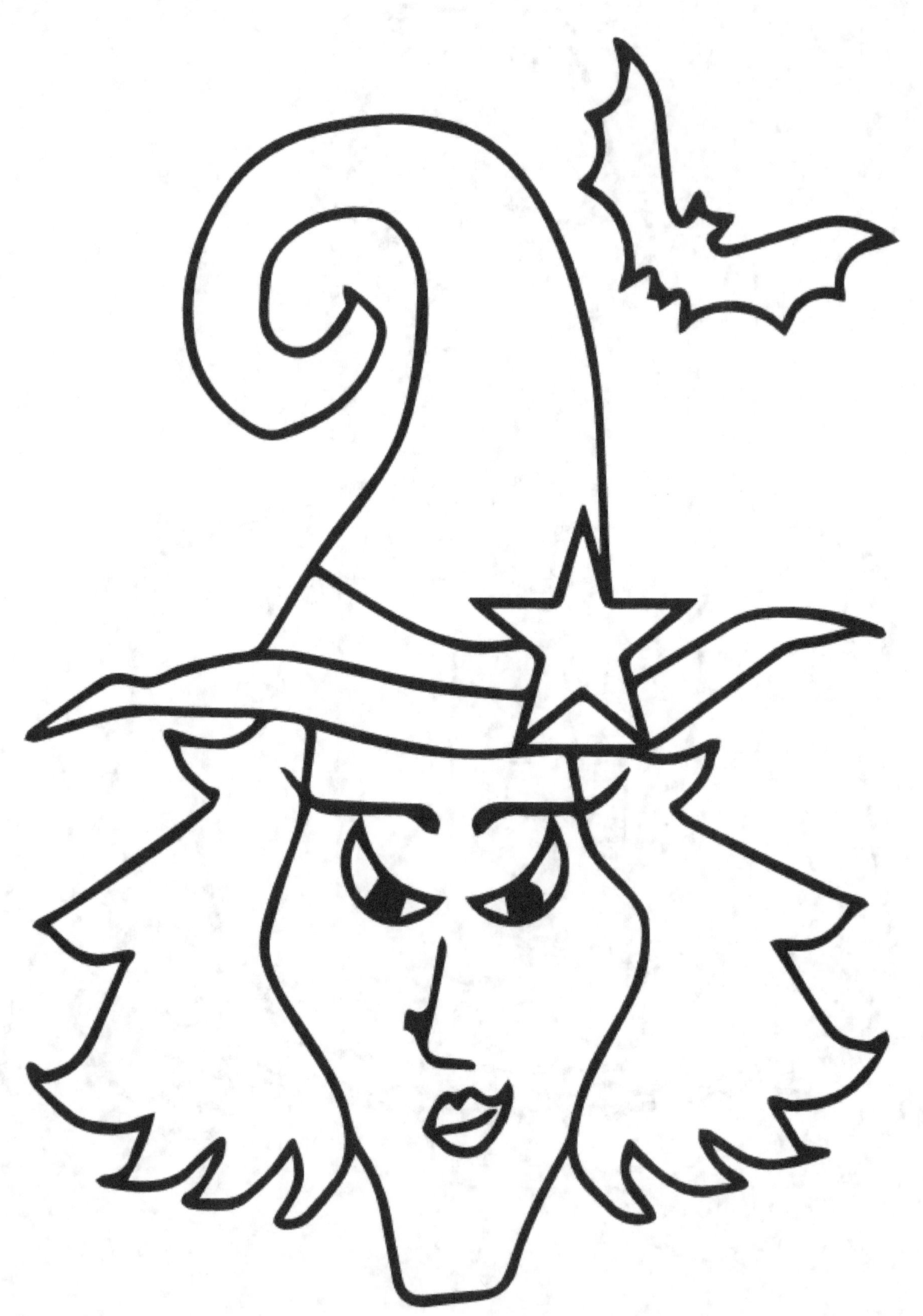

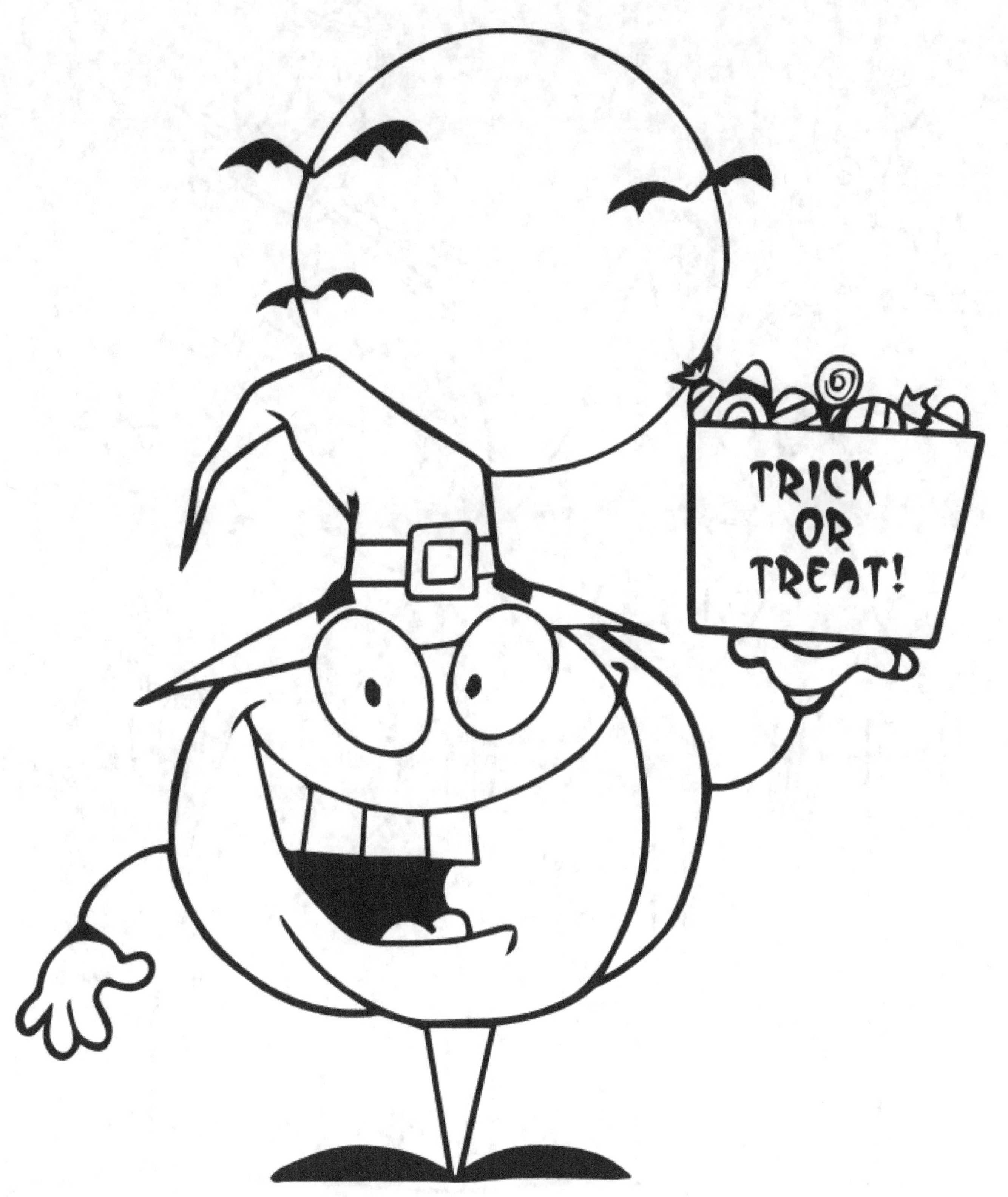

TRICK OR TREAT!

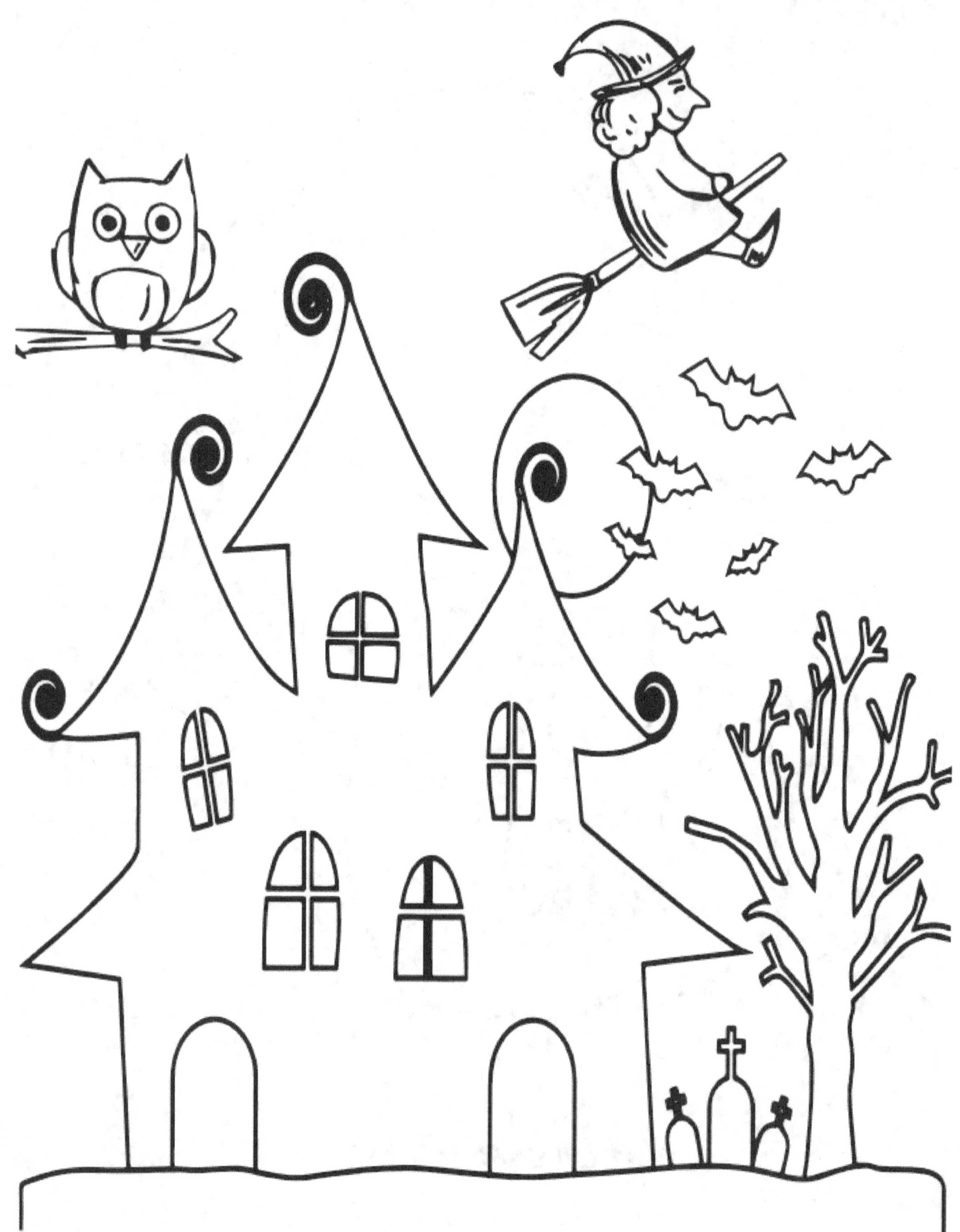

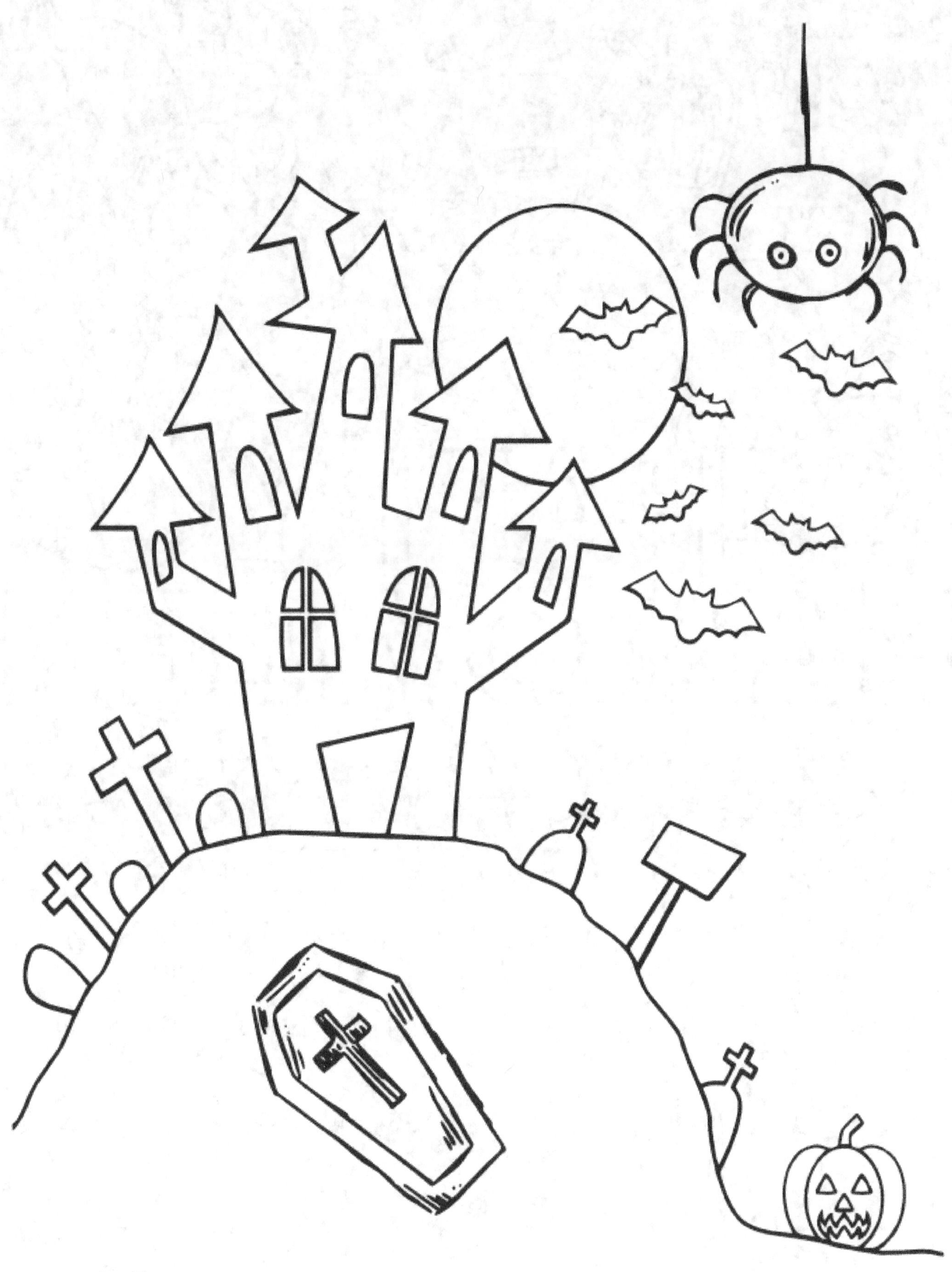

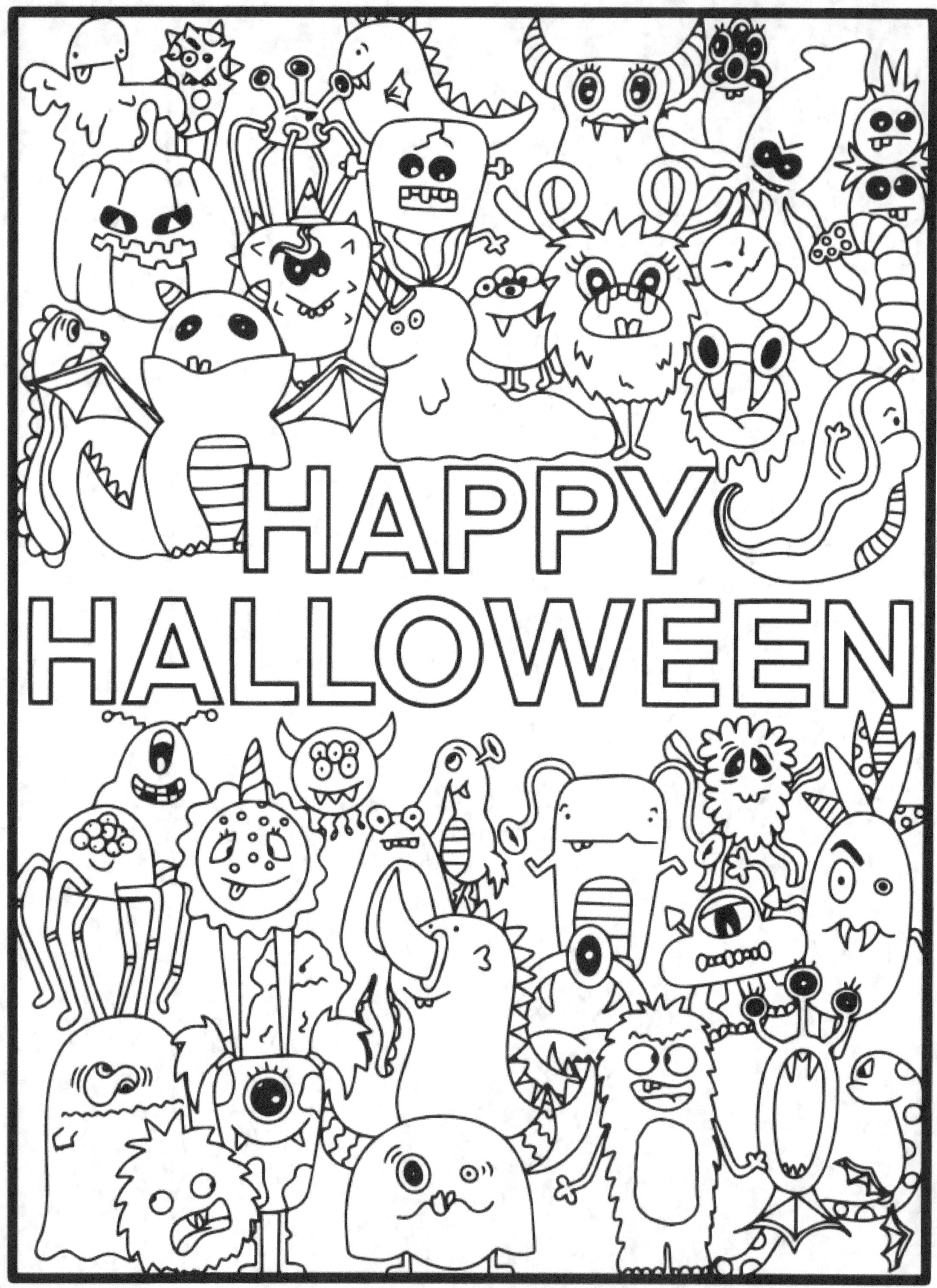

HAPPY
HALLOWEEN

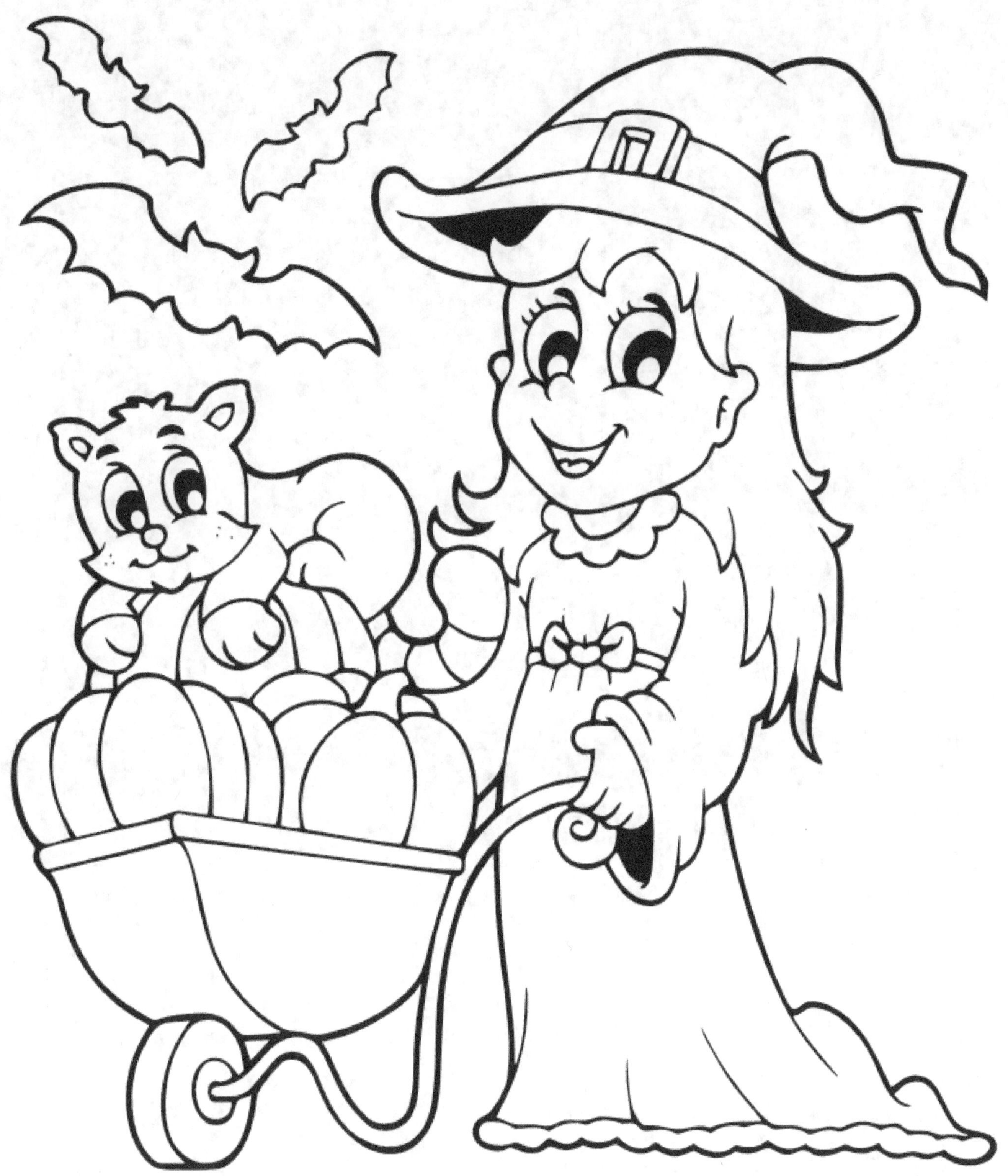